Table of Contents

Preface   vii

Chapter One	The Need for a New Modernism	1
Chapter Two	The Authority of the Bible	31
Chapter Three	Hermeneutics	45
Chapter Four	Seeing through a Glass Darkly	61
Chapter Five	Revisioning God	77
Chapter Six	Christ and Christians	109
Chapter Seven	H. Richard Niebuhr Revisited and Revised	135
Chapter Eight	The Ethics of Capital Punishment	151

Index   167

TOWARD A NEW MODERNISM

Kenneth Cauthen

University Press of America, Inc.
Lanham • New York • London

Copyright © 1997 by
University Press of America,® Inc.
4720 Boston Way
Lanham, Maryland 20706

3 Henrietta Street
London, WC2E 8LU England

All rights reserved
Printed in the United States of America
British Cataloging in Publication Information Available

Library of Congress Cataloging-in-Publication Data

Cauthen, Kenneth.
Toward a new modernism / Kenneth Cauthen.
p. cm.
Includes bibliographical references and Index.
l. Theology. I. Title.
BT80.C35 1996   230'.046--dc20   96-41462 CIP

ISBN 0-7618-0520-6 (cloth: alk. ppr.)
ISBN 0-7618-0521-4 (pbk: alk. ppr.)

∞™ The paper used in this publication meets the minimum
requirements of American National Standard for information
Sciences—Permanence of Paper for Printed Library Materials,
ANSI Z39.48—1984

IN MEMORIAM

John Wilfred Cauthen
June 17, 1907 - May 1, 1995

If God loves us as much as my Father loved me, then we are indeed most fortunate.

Preface

The essays to follow present a theological outlook from a modernist or, perhaps better, a neo-modernist perspective. Following many of the earlier "Chicago school" modernists, a form of theistic naturalism is set forth on the basis of a method that can be described as empirical-rational pragmatism. It assumes a version of thoroughgoing relativism and is suffused with a skepticism that generates a modesty about the conclusions reached. I espouse a doctrine of a limited, opportunistic God who works in and through the *eros* in all life to accomplish the divine aims without interfering with natural law or human freedom. The notion of a God restricted in power is constructed in order to save the divine love, there being no other way known to me adequately to resolve the theodicy question.

A di-polar view of God is elaborated that distinguishes between Uncreated and Created dimensions within Primordial Ultimacy. This view has affinities with process-relational theology, although it is decidedly located on the empirical-pragmatic rather than the rationalistic-speculative wing of that movement. I hold a point of view closer to Bernard Meland, Bernard Loomer, and Henry Nelson Wieman than to Charles Hartshorne or Alfred North Whitehead, although the influence of the latter thinker is visible at nearly every turn. This is theology clearly with an American perspective, with the influence of European modes of thought receding ever more into the distance.

The result is intended to be a Christian perspective, although many will finds its naturalistic tendencies too great a compromise of classical and biblical conceptions of God. Others will find even less promising my view of the Bible and of Jesus as the Christ. Here my modernism is most in evidence. A modernist or neo-modernist takes a stand initially as a self in the world rather than as a believer in the church. The aim is to find a way of belief and habits of practice that provide an understanding of ultimate meaning and a way of coping with life that lead to the fullest actualization of the potential for justice and joy for all. From within that stance one becomes a Christian by finding in that tradition the most propitious grounding for faith and ethics. This is meant in the logical and epistemological sense when reflection about these matters comes into clear self-consciousness. I am aware that historically and existentially I am a Christian because I was reared by Baptists who taught me to believe in this way before I was able to think too much about what I was doing.

What is offered in the Christian way of believing and living is the most excellent if not unsurpassable option available. The norm of all theory, including religious belief, is the best we know up to now from all sources. Chief and central in providing us with the highest and best we know is the biblical witness to Jesus, believed to be the Christ. What is taken from that tradition by modernists is believed to be close to the heart of biblical religion, although the notion of an essence of Christianity is abandoned. It is the centrality of what is appropriated from the Bible that provides the claim of Christian identity for the modernist, although many will find this connection far too tenuous.

One consequence of this way of thinking is that the Bible is neither the norm nor the container of the norm of belief. Moreover, not even Jesus functioning as Christ can be normative in matters of faith and ethics in the strictest sense. All judgments about truth and value are made by persons and groups on the basis of what is most compelling for them here and now. As an individual Christian I decide what is true, right, and good on the basis of what I cannot help but believe, i. e., what I cannot not accept as compelling. The words and deeds of Jesus must be evaluated by persons and groups, by individuals and communities, in the light of the best they know from all sources up to now.

Perhaps the claim most likely to provoke resistance and refutation is that to a large extent this is the way it works in practice, regardless of theological theory that may point to the Bible or to Jesus as the objective norm of religious and ethical truth. I contend that no person or group allows the Bible or even Jesus to teach as the Word of God for today what they know or believe, for whatever reasons, to be either untrue or immoral. Rather we find in the Bible and in Jesus the support for our own way of thinking. Jesus is remade in every theology to fit the image that particular outlook requires. For feminists Jesus is a feminist, for traditionalists Jesus upholds male supremacy, and so on. Christ as a theological concept is a mirror in which we discover our own outlook, recognizing, of course, that the Bible and Jesus are prominent sources of what we profess as truth about God and life. For Christians, the Bible enters centrally into the determination of what is true about God, Christ, humanity, and the world, but the way in which it functions as an authority is decided by the interpreter. The Bible is not self-interpreting, nor does it come with a user's manual.

Topics dealt with in one or more essays include an assessment of contemporary theology, theological method, the authority of the Bible, hermeneutics, language about God, the doctrine of God, theodicy, a way of conceiving Jesus as the Christ, Christian ethics, the ethics of capital punishment, and the meaning of hope.

Chapter One is a call for a new modernism. I review 20th century developments in theology as a background against which I outline what a new modernism might be like and to indicate why I think it would serve a useful purpose to pursue that way of thinking.

Chapters Two, Three, and Four deal with the Bible, its authority, and its interpretation. I suggest why a modernist approach is more helpful than liberal or conservative alternatives. The thesis is that in the final analysis we are the functional authorities. What we claim the Bible teaches as the Word of God for today is identical with our own beliefs about God, value, duty. and the way to the abundant life. Whatever the text may say, the interpreter has the last and definitive word.

In Chapter Five I set forth a doctrine of God constructed as a form of theistic naturalism or naturalistic theism. God is a Cosmic Organism with Uncreated and Created dimensions, whose Body is the World, who may be thought of metaphorically or mythically as a Person. In this version of naturalistic panentheism, God is seen as the Creative, Struggling, Suffering, Loving Ground of the Cosmic Process who originates life in all its forms and seeks to bring all experiencing subjects (organisms) to the highest possible fulfillment of maximized enjoyment. A conception of God, however, must not only account for the positive creativity exhibited in the evolutionary processes but must also be able to explain its dysteleological aspects as well. Evolution in many ways appears to be a blind cruel, and wasteful affair. The problem of evil is explored briefly, and the concept of a God limited in power is adopted. Finally, an empirical philosophy of hope is outlined.

Chapter Six offers the option of viewing our knowledge of Christ pragmatically rather than as the absolutists, the critical realists, and the deconstructionists do. This means that we see our Christologies and the their implications for living as interpretations of the reality of Christ as experienced rather than as objective descriptions thought to correspond with reality. Moreover, Jesus is a source of our ethical values but not their norm. We are the ultimate functional authorities who decide what is true, good, and beautiful based on the best we know up to now from all sources, Jesus being chief among our informants.

Chapter Seven offers a revision of H. Richard Niebuhr's *Christ and Culture* thesis. I propose that strictly speaking we should not speak of Christ *and* culture as if these were two independent factors that constitute opposite poles of a continuum. Rather there is only a Christ *within* culture. Christians can be related to their social and cultural environment in all the five ways Niebuhr has so skillfully worked out. Culture, however, is the all-embracing framework in which both Christ and Christians live and function. A Christ who transcends or is independent of culture in this sense cannot be found. Jesus was a cultural being, and all conceptions of Christ are clothed in cultural garb. Jesus was the product of his history and culture, however much he may have creatively refashioned it, although whether a single idea he proposed was entirely original is questionable. Culture is the context in which we know Christ, interpret Christ, and obey Christ. This way of conceiving of Christ assumes and carries forth the epistemology adumbrated in the previous chapter.

In the final chapter, I offer a brief summary of Christian ethics based on the key principle of *unconditional mutual love*. I show how this norm can be interpreted in dealing with capital punishment. I make use of a distinction between the ethical and the ecstatic dimensions of love, and I contend that Christian love has a justice dimension. I maintain that *agape* is not sacrificial in essence, although it may become so contextually when the neighbor's need exceeds our own or when the greater good of the community requires it. Central to the whole discussion is a delineation of the spheres within which each of these dimensions of Christian ethics is relevant.

Throughout I have assumed a formal and a material norm for my own version of the Christian vision. The formal norm is the best we know from all sources up to now. The material norm is the love of God shown to us and the love of God and neighbor required of us as the religious and moral ideal for life.

Such are the main themes of these essays. Of the seven, three in an earlier form have been previously published in journals. The fact that the individual chapters were originally prepared independently of each other makes for more repetition than is desirable, but I hope this feature will not detract from the impact of the whole. Taken all together they constitute a distinctive outlook on the contemporary scene, I believe. They occupy the same general ideological territory as that marked out by those who typically publish articles in the *American Journal of Theology and Philosophy*, in which Chapter One originally appeared. Chapters Four and Seven were first published in *Encounter*. In addition, parts of Chapters One and Five are also found in my *Theological Biology*, published by Edwin Mellen Press. I am grateful for the permission given me to use this material in these essays. They are offered for whatever edification they may provide to readers and are intended to provoke both discussion and refutation -- the sort that may lead to greater depth of understanding and a more acute rendering of matters of importance to all who seek to know truth and to do good.

Kenneth Cauthen
Rochester, NY
July 3, 1996

Chapter One

The Need for a New Modernism[1]

Contemporary theology stands in need of a new modernism. It would be useful in this regard to resume the path that was being followed by some branches of American liberal thought when attention turned in most quarters to an emerging neo-orthodoxy. I refer specifically to the modernistic liberals, many of whom were part of the "Chicago school." These theologians explicitly defined themselves as modern intellectuals informed by empirical sciences and historical disciplines that thoroughly undermined the Protestant orthodoxy of their youth and called for a radical rethinking of the Christian message. Without such a reconstruction Christianity would cease to be credible and important for life in the 20th century. They assumed that all social systems and conceptual schemes are historically relative and culturally conditioned. Religious

---

[1] This chapter was published in an earlier form in *American Journal of Theology and Philosophy* (January, 1992), 1-22. Used by permission.

doctrines serve a practical function of relating us to whatever in the cosmos has saving power. Yet these thoroughly modern relativists and pragmatists also stood in the Christian tradition, believing that it contained permanent values that could be reclaimed.[1]

This essay will examine some developments in contemporary American theology that create the opportunity and need for a new modernism. I will concentrate particularly on (1) questions of method and authority and (2) the reality and activity of God. In the light of a critical evaluation of major schools of present-day thought I will outline the shape of a new modernism.

THE TWENTIETH-CENTURY BACKGROUND

The call for a thorough recasting of ancient ways of thinking has, of course, been a common theme within theology since the Enlightenment and is the defining characteristic of liberal Christian thought.[2] The evangelical liberals, however, claimed to recapture the heart of the ancient Gospel in modern categories. So did the neo-orthodox thinkers. So also do many present-day process, black, feminist, and liberation theologians. The modernistic liberals of the Chicago school, however, took a more radical stance. They gave up the notion of an identifiable Christian essence persisting throughout all its historical forms. For Shailer Mathews, Christianity was whatever it had become over the long centuries of its development. A Christian is anyone who professes loyalty to Jesus. The modernists vowed to re-present as binding on contemporary belief only what is valuable to the present age as that is judged by contemporary criteria. Scientific methods of inquiry into nature and history provided for them the most reliable form of knowledge about the source of human good.

The overly optimistic estimate of human possibilities associated with liberal theology (along with other factors) produced a revulsion against it. Many of its typical themes -- the immanence of God, confidence in science and human progress, emphasis on experience as the source of religious truth, a focus on the historical Jesus -- were abandoned in neo-orthodoxy. Discontinuity replaced continuity as the central informing motif. Paradox, ambiguity, and tension replaced liberal harmony and rational unity. In neo-orthodoxy attention shifted from autonomous reason and human possibilities to God's self-initiated self-disclosure in certain crucial events of salvation history. Divine revelation judged and contradicted cultural wisdom, so that a leap of faith is required to appropriate it. Jesus was no longer primarily the moral example and spiritual ideal to be emulated. Emphasis was put on the Christ-event -- the paradox of the God-man. Jesus embodied God's Word of grace to sinful humanity. The Bible had authority as the decisive witness to divine revelation, although it was interpreted by liberal methods. Augustine, Luther, and Calvin -- generally scorned by liberals -- were warmly embraced because they affirmed the transcendence of God, the depravity of humanity, and salvation by grace. These themes spoke powerfully to a civilization whose foundations had been shaken, reeling and rocking from the massive evils of the first half of the 20th century.[3]

The revival of orthodoxy was incorporated into a more humane post-Enlightenment framework that rejected many of its repulsive aspects. The inheritance of depravity and the damnation of non-elect children had no standing. Established findings of empirical science and of historical criticism were affirmed. Classical doctrines of creation, incarnation, and consummation were regarded as myths to be taken "seriously but not literally" (Reinhold Niebuhr). Hence, American neo-orthodoxy was, in these respects, a thoroughly modern theological outlook. The aim of speaking to the present age was so strong in Reinhold Niebuhr, Paul Tillich, and Rudolf Bultmann that they could also be called neo-liberal.[4]

While neo-orthodoxy served its generation well by bringing good news to a bad news generation, theology needs to take a different direction today. Difficulties in contemporary American theology also justify a call for a new modernism. Two problems will be highlighted: (1) the question of method and authority and (2) the reality and activity of God.

THE AUTHORITY QUESTION

A variety of outlooks since 1960 -- most prominently, black, feminist, and process theologies -- shifted attention away from the neo-orthodox theme of recovering the "message" of the Bible. The new focus was on the "situation" to which the Gospel is to be addressed and on human experience as a source of theology.[5] This is a relative distinction, since all modern theologies want to be both biblical and relevant. Another relative distinction is between those perspectives that focus on the particularities of somebody's experience (some specific groups and individuals) and those that base their thinking on the universalities of everybody's experience (all individuals and groups). Black and feminist perspectives exemplify the former, while process theologies are examples of the latter. Making experience the starting point is a stance shared with the older liberals. Some black theologians, however, spoke with a neo-orthodox accent blended with a reliance on the history and culture of black Christians.[6] The early theology of hope espoused by Jürgen Moltmann continued to base theology on the Word of God.[7] Process theologies, however, are more neo-liberal. They refer to universal human experience as a source of truth that can be harmonized with the crucial biblical theme of a God of unbounded love who is affected by and responsive to events in time and history.[8] Other revisionist theologians, assuming a self-conscious identity as secular modern persons, have sought to correlate the meanings contained in classic Christian texts with interpretations of common human experience.[9]

Revisionist methodology unites classic Christian motifs with modernity but sees the results as a defensible synthesis that transforms both ancient orthodoxy and modern secularism. Process theologies, for example, contradict notions of divine omnipotence and eliminate use of coercive power to fulfill the divine purpose. Revisionists want to be biblical like the neo-orthodox and modern like the liberals. Yet, as defined by David Tracy, it is philosophical reason that finally determines what truth claims are valid. That is a modernist theme, although the older liberals believed in the harmony of revelation and reason. Revisionists appear to be evangelically liberal or neo-orthodox in claiming to re-present from the classical texts what is central and vital to those ancient authorities.[10] Hence, Tracy-type revisionism appears to be on the boundary between a liberal/neo-orthodox and a modernist outlook.

What, then, is to guarantee either the Christian or the secular character of the result if each transforms the other? It is the interpreter, of course, who makes this happen. By eliciting the meanings found in Christian texts and in common human experience and then doing the testing, a particular theologian can practically guarantee a valid outcome! Theologies are true to the Gospel and pertinent to the situation only as somebody judges them to be so. No revisioning will satisfy everybody. Pluralism is inescapable and can only be partially and never satisfactorily overcome. This does not negate the considerable overlapping that occurs among the many circles of interpretation whose centers may be close to each other.[11] Some revisionists and other thinkers appear to be moving closer to the new modernism I advocate.[12]

Tracy and others champion the need for a "public theology." Public means an appeal to what is reasonable within the framework of contemporary secular consciousness. Rules of evidence established by the various university disciplines must be followed. Theologians cannot appeal to the Bible or a particular tradition of thought as warrants for their claims. They must argue for them on the basis of public sources and norms of truth. Common human experience is the point of reference. Ruled out are statements of the form "X is true because the Bible (or the Pope or the creed, etc.) says so, period." This establishes criteria specific enough to eliminate Christian tradition or the cultural reason of other societies or epochs as intrinsically authoritative. It is sufficiently general, however, to permit a wide variety of fundamentally conflicting claims based on reason and common human experience. Accepting the "morality of scientific reason" might persuade biologists, psychologists, sociologists, and philosophers to admit theologians to the conversation. Even if Bibles are left at home when they go to the seminar, however, will theologians convince any non-believers with their rational God-talk and with their assurances that they too are university intellectuals, one of them at heart? How far does being secular and reasonable take theology in practical terms toward a wider audience? Which public does theology take into account in announcing its warrants and making its claims? To which contemporary philosopher does the theologian turn for a reasonable interpretation of common human experience -- Ayer, Russell, Heidegger, Sartre, Whitehead, Dewey, Derrida, Rorty, or Woody Allen? Can philosophy or theology add anything to the description of matters of fact not discoverable by scientific methods of inquiry? Contemporary cultural reason is divided on this crucial question. The metaphysical philosophy advocated by Tracy as his instrument of going public with theology is rejected out of hand by large segments of the secular intellectual community to which he would speak.

Tracy holds that warrants employed by public theology are available in principle to all reasonable persons, although in fact everybody reasons from within particular traditions and communities.[13] He provides no resolution of this predicament. There is, in fact, no universally satisfactory way for theology to be both "public" in appealing to contemporary rational criteria and "confessional" in witnessing to the Gospel. No consensus exists in culture regarding what is reasonable as descriptions of reality and no agreement is present in the church about what is essential to Christian witness. Tracy, like everybody else, is caught in the dilemma posed by the desire for objectivity and universality in the search for truth and the fact of particularity and relativity that divides humanity into a plurality of competing communities.

The modernist is more consistently pluralist, particularist, and relativist. Public theology is a neither a rational nor a theological necessity. Its pragmatic success rate is limited. It is a preference and a choice for which good reasons can be given. But it is not demanded by necessary principles of rationality obvious to all reasonable persons. Christian theologians do not even agree among themselves about the sources and norms of religious truth. Whose or which theology are we to offer unbelievers? The post-liberals represented by George Lindbeck, Hans Frei, and the Yale school of theology think that the revisionist way is more likely to compromise the Gospel than to persuade worldly thinkers.[14] Can Tracy show by reason that Karl Barth was wrong in appealing to the Word of God as the norm of Christian truth? Will reasoning with atheists provide a higher conversion rate than quoting Scripture to them? I doubt it. Nevertheless, it is doubtful that any two world-views -- Christian and otherwise -- constitute circles totally outside each other. Hence, meaningful conversation can, if enough good will is assumed, take place among thinkers of radically diverse traditions of thought that may produce widening areas of mutual understanding. Consensus on certain points may exist or be eventually attained. On rare occasions conversion to other points of view may occur. At no point, even assuming universal agreement, is certainty about ultimate matters of fact guaranteed.

John Cobb believes that the universal element in Jesus the Christ is the principle and process of "creative transformation," by which a way of life is converted by confrontation with new and better insights into truth, value, and good practice. He urges representatives of the various historic religions to become radically open to the truth that the other might offer. His hope is that this process of mutual conversion will in time lead to new ways of thinking and living not embodied in any past religious tradition or sacred writing.[15] This might in fact happen if done with enough dedication and integrity, although I am more pessimistic than Cobb about the prospects of discovering some fundamental new, soul-grabbing truth about existence not dreamed of in past or present. Moreover, there is the tricky question as to how we know which transformations are "creative" rather than neutral or destructive. Since "creative transformation" defines a general formal process void of particular content, don't we need some criterion to judge the results of its operation in practice? Indeed, he does find this principle incarnate in the words, deeds, and person of Jesus, but it cannot be formulated in specific doctrines, creeds, or any particular set of theological beliefs or ethical values. Rather Jesus creatively transformed whatever he encountered, and this is his meaning and significance. The only way Cobb could refer to some material or content-norm found in the biblical witness to Christ would be to reopen the type of liberal "essence of Christianity" question that he has abandoned.

He could, of course, say that we make the judgment here and now on the basis of the best we know up to now from all sources, in which case he joins the modernists. My impression is that his project was intended to transcend these options. He wants a universal Christ incarnate in a particular Jesus, loyalty to whom is compatible with a religious pluralism that avoids relativism. It is not clear that even the process of "creative transformation" can work this miracle.

Black and feminist perspectives have been particularistic, centering on the experience of blacks and of women respectively.[16] Yet they claim to have found in the liberation motif the authentic Christian message. Liberation theologians tend to assume the truth of the Gospel and focus on its power to emancipate the oppressed. Black and feminist theologians, however, confront the fact that oppressive practices like slavery and the subordination of women are present without condemnation in many places in both the Hebrew Bible and the New Testament. Liberation theologians find little comfort for their enterprise in the Book of Joshua that has Yahweh directing an enterprise against the Canaanites that reminds us of the assault Europeans carried out against Native Americans. Judges might be a candidate for the liberation canon, since it recounts numerous episodes of emancipation. However, the reason given for the oppression of Israel was their apostasy. Only subjugation that is not deserved is a proper theme for purposes of liberation thought. Moreover, it is not self-evident that liberation in the Bible is always the same thing contemporary black and feminist theologies are talking about. Liberation theologies are frequently obscure or ambiguous about how liberation, as they conceive it, relates to liberation and the means of achieving it found in Scripture. Liberation theologians call upon the poor and oppressed to organize themselves for purposes of overthrowing the oppressors. Is there even one instance in Scripture in which the poor and oppressed are urged to assume responsibility for their own worldly destiny and to engage in revolutionary social-political revolt for the sake of establishing an equalitarian secular order? In the deliverance of the Israelites from Egypt, God did the liberating, not the people acting on their own behalf.

In the New Testament liberation is primarily from sin and death, not from various forms of political and social oppression. Deliverance from the evils of this life is achieved fully only at the Endtime consummation when all of nature as well as society will be perfected by a new creative act of God. When an apocalyptic outlook reigns, liberation (and that word alone is inadequate to describe biblical hope) occurs only in a divinely coerced cosmic transformation. Contemporary theologians want economic, social, and political justice in this world. They want it fully and now or as soon as possible, not in some sweet by and by that keeps getting put off further into the future. The deliverance of Israel from Egyptian slavery was a social liberation event. Yet neither in the wilderness nor in Canaan was life all that happy, prosperous, or free.

In any case, liberation theologians do not expect that release from oppression will be accompanied by the kind of supernatural intervention that rescued Israel from the Pharaoh. Moreover, Israel continued to be oppressed periodically and eventually nearly all the time. Nor were the magnificent predictions of the new Isaiah(s) (Is.40-66) of a New Creation fulfilled in the post-Exilic period. The apocalyptic expectations of the New Testament never came to pass. Rev. 21 is not what black and feminist theologians want most. This is not to deny that secular social justice is a prominent theme in the Hebrew Bible, less so in the New Testament. Nevertheless, liberties are taken in redefining liberation in more systemic, sociological terms than the New Testament in particular will sustain. That contemporary liberation theologies represent a valid modernizing of basic biblical motifs is thoroughly convincing to me. That they merely *re*-present the heart of the Bible in its own terms is claiming too much.

To find the ultimate liberation event and paradigm in the resurrected Christ, as Cone does,[17] is to engage in the kind of spiritualizing and transcendentalizing that liberation theologies object to in other perspectives. The social order following the resurrection remained full of suffering and injustice and still does. To reinterpret the consummation referred to by the apostolic witness as yet to come, as fundamentalist, neo-orthodox, eschatological, and liberation theologies routinely do, may be a theological necessity. The result hardly qualifies as a *re*-presentation of what the Bible says. To reinterpret the time-frame of the promised consummation in the radical way required is a commonplace. The usual claim is that this is a minor point incidental to the essence. If such a drastic recasting of biblical assumptions is undertaken to accommodate the historical facts and the modern consciousness, what is the crucial sense in which the product can be said to be biblical? At what point does reconstruction become destruction? And must not the truth-claims of the new eschatology be judged by reason, since the Bible's own definition of what liberation means has already been discarded?

That the New Testament message must be restated within a modern framework is, of course, a familiar claim in post-Enlightenment theology. However, the reinterpretation needed is more fundamental than many contemporary thinkers who would be both Christian and modern acknowledge. Methodological integrity is threatened unless the hermeneutical procedures explicitly adopted allow or require a reconstruction as thoroughgoing as that actually performed.

James Cone asserts that the two measuring rods of black theology are Christ and black liberation. He unites these, of course, by rejecting interpretations of Christ contrary to black liberation.[18] Cone strongly affirms the particularity, subjectivity, and relativity of all theology. He chastises white theologians for claiming objectivity. Yet in the end he affirms that the liberating theme defines *the* objective Gospel and is not merely a specific concrete norm for a given situation. The poor and oppressed are empistemologically privileged. The non-oppressed cannot challenge such a claim. So once again, despite all the affirmations of the relativity of all human efforts, it is maintained that a particular interpretation has grasped the objective truth of faith. Of course, specific forms of liberation theology are acknowledged by him to be limited, partial, and in need of revision. He readily allows that the many stories of the afflicted must be reformed in light of the one Story. In the end, however, Cone does not go beyond the familiar neo-orthodox framework that assumes a Christological canon within the canon, an abstractable vital core that can take various conceptual forms. For all his flirting with radical particularity and relativity,[19] he -- like nearly everybody else -- in the end purports to know the normative content of Scripture. All non-liberating views are heretical. Either they miss the point or are distorted by the social location and interests of their adherents and thus are wrong. Calvin, Luther, Harnack, and Rauschenbusch all played "at last, we've got it." Cone plays it too. A pluralist, relativist, and pragmatist asks: Is liberation theology as he understands it one plausible modern reading, or has he discovered the universal Gospel residing in an internally self-defined form in the Bible itself?[20]

Some post-Christian feminists like Mary Daly have declared Christianity too thoroughly rotten to be salvaged.[21] Christian feminists find their position ambiguous. Much of the Bible and nearly all of Christian tradition is deeply infused with beliefs and practices oppressive of women. It is especially difficult for evangelicals to have their Bible and their feminism too without being more modernist than their view of scriptural authority allows.[22] Many liberal feminists are candid enough to say that the norm is "whatever contributes to the liberation of women." If the Bible contributes to the full realization of the humanity of women, well and good. If not, only what is in harmony with that norm will be retained. Modernists applaud that procedure, although the liberation of women is not the whole or sole content of saving truth.

Rosemary Ruether uses the "prophetic-liberating tradition" to judge everything else in Scripture. She finds an egalitarian motif that stresses justice and fulfillment for all as an undercurrent and as a "repressed tradition" in the New Testament. This cornerstone becomes the basis for a critique of patriarchy and is the clue to a normative Gospel centering on equality, mutuality, and deliverance from all systems that exalt one group over another.[23] Christianity in none of its forms, however, can be regarded as absolute or final. Other ancient religious and modern secular traditions can also inform feminine consciousness. The final or culture-transcending norm for all religions, cultural traditions, and philosophies is "whatever is liberating and fulfilling for women" within a vision only partly derived from Scripture. She uses a criterion arising in contemporary consciousness to criticize all traditions. She acknowledges that the Bible and Christian history are dominated by patriarchy. Since she regards as authoritative in Scripture only what meets her own critical criteria, I call her in that regard a modernist. Taking into account all that she says, she appears to be suspended ambiguously between liberalism/neo-orthodoxy and modernism.

Elisabeth Schüssler Fiorenza is closer to a modernist perspective. She positions herself between the neo-orthodox essence-accident scheme of Ruether and the post-Christian philosophy of Daly.[24] Nevertheless, she appears still to espouse a notion of biblical truth and revelation that defines *the* Gospel for everybody.[25] She goes behind the texts to locate communities of faith and practice whose ethos becomes the norm of all traditions, including Scripture. She finds in early Christian history groups who practice a liberating, equalitarian religion of mutuality and justice -- a women's church whose praxis is a discipleship of equals. By recovering what has been obscured by the dominant patriarchal traditions, she locates something normative incarnate in history. She finds it in a religious movement loyal to Jesus, the founder and exemplar of the faith. How does she know that it is the liberating-equalitarian- mutuality ethos that is truly definitive of *ecclesia*? Her modern feminist consciousness tells her so. She recognizes that the Bible is predominantly sexist in its textual expression.

Her claim, of course, is that women's egalitarian church embodies the truth, the way, and the life exemplified in Jesus and his earliest disciples. In that sense she is "liberal" in the tradition of Adolf Harnack, who identified the "essence" with its original formulation in the historical Jesus. How sure can we be that any contemporary reconstruction of Jesus is reliable enough to make such a claim? Can we deny that this may be another idealized and modernized Jesus mistaken for the real one? Whether Jesus' calling forth a discipleship of equals involved a self-conscious attack on patriarchy as defined by a present-day critical feminist outlook is contestable, as she notes.[26] It is arguable that the egalitarian motifs in early Christianity are best understood in eschatological and ecclesiastical terms. They do not necessarily imply imperatives for reforming the existing secular social order. And does it not require a considerable imaginative leap to identify a small sectarian-utopian-eschatological community in the Roman Empire with the situation of women, especially white, middle-class, affluent ones, in the United States today?

To maintain that a critical feminist consciousness calling for full equality of the sexes in every aspect of secular and church life is a valid modernizing of the *praxis* of Jesus and of some early Christian communities is one thing. Modernists applaud that move. To claim that this contemporary outlook is identical with the liberating-egalitarian tradition in the New Testament is something else and not beyond question. Why not say that we appropriate from the Christian past only what is best and worthy of preservation? Why worry whether we have discovered its foundational heart and soul? It is important, of course, to get the history of the early church correct for its own sake. Would it matter normatively whether there ever was a women's church existing as a discipleship of equals surrounding Jesus? This is a different question from whether or not such a church was a historical fact.

For Ruether and Schüssler Fiorenza, then, Scripture is authoritative only in so far as it exhibits or conforms to the standard dictated by a modern critical feminine consciousness. They do not hesitate to reject outright anything that does not pass this test. The functioning norm for them is defined in the light of present-day reason and experience. Else how would they know to recognize those elements that are liberating for women as the real Gospel when they find it Scripture or in early Christian practice? Yet they claim they are not inventing the content and norm of religious truth but finding it in Jesus and thus in the Bible or in early church communities.[27] Mary Daly stated the implicit logic of much liberal feminism in saying that she is a feminist, whether Jesus was or not.[28] That is a modernist principle. Liberals, however, want their feminism and Jesus too.[29]

Sheila Greeve Davaney maintains that Ruether, Schüssler Fiorenza, as well as Mary Daly, apparently hold on to a correspondence theory of truth, at least for their own positions. Yet they otherwise recognize the conditioned nature of all human thought and social practice.[30] All three assume that "what is liberating and fulfilling for women" is the operating norm for judging all traditions past and present. They also profess that truth so measured puts us in touch with Ultimate Reality. For this reason Davaney contends that they have failed to carry through the full implications of a modern historical consciousness. Such consciousness recognizes the relativity of all human thought whatsoever, not excluding feminist or any other kind of liberation theology. If this is the case, they are not modernist as defined by the pluralist, relativist, and pragmatic outlook advocated on these pages.

Trying to find texts and/or principles that make sexual equality appear to be the real biblical view is unnecessary. Feminists don't need the Bible to tell them they are equal with men. We rightly reject those passages that teach subordination. Why should we take so much comfort in the few that do teach equality or use feminist images for God? Besides Paul may have only meant in Gal. 3:27-28 that women and men, slaves and free persons, are equal in status before God. He may not have implied that equality is a principle for organizing secular society. At the same time, the New Testament proclaims that eschatological redemption is available to men and women alike. Many New Testament writings assume slavery and the subordination of women (Ephes. 5: 21-33, 6:5-9; Col. 3:18-25; I Tim. 2:11-25; Titus 2:5; Philemon; I Peter 2:13-3:7). Unless we are prepared to argue that these views are justified contextually, we have to say that the Bible is wrong on those points. In any case, the social situation of early Christians -- an underclass of apocalyptic sectarians devoid of political power -- differs far too much from that of contemporary Americans to make direct identity plausible. Women are equal with men, and a sexually one-sided view of God is inadequate for today, whether the Bible agrees or not.[31] Truth as we judge it is what operationally matters. In the last analysis we determine what is authoritative in Scripture. Whatever in Scripture appears to be either untrue, immoral, or irrelevant, we reject (or ignore), whether we are fundamentalists, liberals, or modernists.

In short, much that is compelling in contemporary theology is in agreement with the modernist outlook. (1) Weakness appears in the aspiration for a public theology that can be both biblical and acceptable to the secular consciousness of university elites with broadly effective results. The aim is commendable. However, no consensus exists about biblical religion in the church or about reason and reality in the university. Hence, no generally productive consequences necessarily follow from the program of public theology. All useful conversations between theology and other accounts of the ultimate facts are local, particular, and aim at some temporary practical accommodation. No global prescriptions defining the task of theologians in relation to the methods and conclusions of other reasoning professionals will find universal acceptance today. (2) The other shortcoming appears when theologians identify their normative belief systems with the universal Gospel defined by Scripture or Jesus. It is time to give up the search for the essence of Christianity or at least to forego the claim of having found it. Modern theologians always manage to interpret the essential tenets of Scripture in ways that do not offend their own modern consciousness and their denial of supernatural phenomena. Both these deficiencies spring from overconfidence in the power of theological reason to find something universal, or at least objectively reliable, either in revelation or in reason to which the weary soul can repair amidst the confusions and calamities of the modern world. We have to be more modest and particular in our efforts and settle for something less than certainty. Pluralism and relativism, if taken with the seriousness that many contemporary theologians themselves initially recognize, will push theology toward a new modernism.

THE ACTIVITY OF GOD

Difficulties arise also with respect to the reality and activity of God. Speaking of the acts of God in nature and history -- central to the Bible -- has been problematic since the Enlightenment. The assumptions underlying classical theology scarcely allowed room for human actions that originate novelty.[32] Nor do human actions set the course of history in a fashion not overruled by the sovereign will of God. Nothing determines matters of fact and destiny in the final analysis but the omnipotent divine will. Moreover, belief in miracles gave genuine substance to the notion of "the mighty acts of God."

Liberal theologies for the most part gave up the idea of supernatural intervention. Liberalism was bound to ideas of a law-abiding universe and thus lacked the idea of miracle. By emphasizing the immanence of God, they saw in the course of nature and history evidences of divine aim. The liberal view identified the providence of God with a general purposive dimension in things. The idea that God did specific things on particular occasions, like rolling back the waters of the Red Sea or raising the dead, disappeared. Also, the fact of human autonomy in originating events required the cooperation of humanity to bring about the gradual coming of the kingdom of God on earth.

Neo-orthodoxy substituted transcendence for liberal immanence but retained respect for scientific ways of accounting for events in nature and history. Thus, miracle played no more role than in liberalism (with a few exceptions like Barth).[33] Neo-orthodoxy spoke of "the mighty acts of God" but required heavy use of paradox, myth, symbol, and what amounted to double-talk to make it work. Langdon Gilkey demonstrated that in many cases reference to acts of God, by which connection was made with biblical thought, was brave rhetoric well-nigh empty of content. It was certainly not what Calvin had it mind![34] Since both liberal and neo-orthodox theologies made a place -- as orthodoxy typically had not -- for human freedom as the originating source of novelty and thus of the direction of world history, ideas of providence and eschatology became problematic.[35] It was no longer clear how God's will could be accomplished in all things if human acts set the course of history or if contingent events occurred in nature. Of course, one can always appeal to mystery, asserting that God is somehow ruling in all things although we don't know how. Liberals had confidence that the spirit of Jesus would gradually rule human motives. Progress in kingdom-building was expected, although World War I dampened the optimism of most. Neo-orthodox views of human sinfulness had no such confidence and looked, as Reinhold Niebuhr did, beyond history for the full reign of love and justice. Even then it would require a fresh and presumably unilateral coercive act of God to bring heaven into being. In that sense Niebuhr was orthodox.[36] Generally, however, he was liberal in not believing that God did particular public and visible things here and now. Rather God is the Ultimate Source and End of all things who judges, forgives, and guides human actions. History in its concreteness is the product of human choices and deeds.

In contemporary thought equally formidable problems exist, if present-day thought intends to re-present biblical modes of thought. Process theology by using the technical vocabulary of Whitehead can say precisely how God is active in every event. However, divine activity lacks the irresistible efficacy that both the Bible and orthodox theology asserted without hesitation. Moreover, God's power to overcome evil is limited, requiring human cooperation to make it effective.[37] The process model is more respectful of human freedom and expresses the creative-responsive love of God more credibly to the contemporary mind than classical thought. Nevertheless, it is a departure from notions of divine sovereignty found in the Bible and orthodoxy. Hence, it strains the point to insist that the result is a mere "re-presentation" of that ancient witness. That miracle is accomplished only by proceeding as if what does not fit the contemporary model is not essential.[38] Moreover, in its rationalistic and boldly speculative varieties, the claims of process thought to know so much about the inner workings of God are overconfident. The purists among the main-line process thinkers promise secular skeptics and that if only they will buy into the metaphysics of Whitehead, belief in a robust, biblically compatible theism will become credible. Unfortunately, the difficulties posed by taking *Process and Reality* literally are no less forbidding than those associated with belief in the God of the Bible, except that Whitehead is himself a modern who rules out supernatural divine interventions.

Liberation and eschatological theologies speak of God as the liberator of the oppressed. Yet non-conservative exponents perpetuate liberal and neo-orthodox modes of thought with respect to the priority given to science in explaining the causality that works in nature and history. Thus, they too reject miracle in the old-fashioned sense, except for the resurrection of Jesus. Langdon Gilkey has shown how dubious are the efforts of Wolfhart Pannenberg and Jürgen Moltmann to establish the historicity of the resurrection on grounds of a modern rationality.[39] Such arguments, by and large, convince only those who need no convincing. John Cobb confesses perplexity to know what Moltmann means when he speaks of an ultimate liberation at the consummation.[40] James Cone admits that black theology has no answer to W. R. Jones' question as to why blacks in America are still oppressed after all these centuries.[41]

Liberation theologians do not generally promise the oppressed that a new deliverance from the Pharaohs of today will be accomplished by divinely-sent plagues and wonders similar to those that occurred at the Red Sea. They also give status to human freedom and activity as the real creator of structures of oppression. Thus, it is not clear how God acts to overcome such structures. Presumably God does not interfere with natural law and must work through human freedom, at least here and now. Divine persuasion generally is not effective in securing release of captives from Pharaohs, especially in the short run. Moltmann teaches that God acted supernaturally to raise Christ from the dead as a foretaste of a future supernatural act at the consummation when the world will be made whole. In the present, believers live in memory and hope between these two mighty acts and expend themselves in love to bring about justice and reconciliation.[42] No promise of supernatural help in the present task is offered. God's action in the present apparently consists in inspiring believers through the power of divine promise to liberate the captives and to heal the wounds of the afflicted. Liberation theology is often not precise about how the acts of God and the acts of people are related. Whatever role the Holy Spirit plays does no violence to natural law. Thus, there is vagueness about what is meant with respect to how *God* liberates as something other than human beings doing God's will in bringing about gains in freedom and equality. Do they, indeed, mean something other than that? God has acted and will act in the structures of cosmic and historical events. Now God acts through the promise of future deliverance to generate militant hope and action to emancipate the captives.

In short, many of the same problems of neo-orthodoxy can be found in present-day thought. Frequently interest in technical problems of interpretation -- what Reinhold Niebuhr called "the niceties of pure theology" -- is lacking. The result is that brave talk about the liberating God and of liberating acts of God is in danger of becoming empty rhetoric. Often such speech has little specifiable or precise content in relation to the events of world history, at least of the kind that newspapers report.

Even among theologians who do work at the problem technically, the main result is to demonstrate how difficult the issues are. Contrary theories eliminate each other right and left. It is well-nigh impossible to get agreement about the matter.[43] Once (1) the notion of divine determinism is surrendered and (2) human freedom is made the source of history's content and direction and (3) a law-abiding concept of finite reality is espoused, it becomes extremely difficult to specify how God can do particular things in nature and human events. To forego that option and identify the providence of God with a general outworking of purpose in and through the whole network of finite events may be a theological necessity.[44] I agree that it is. However, it hardly qualifies as a restatement statement of biblical doctrine except in some attenuated sense.

THE SHAPE OF A NEW MODERNISM

In summary, whether we examine the question of the authority of the Bible or inquire into theological language about the reality and activity of God, severe problems arise. Those who would be modern *and* biblical are in danger of betraying one interest or the other. It is time to give up the pretense of merely re-presenting some vital core of biblical thought, some universal Gospel, in contemporary terms. A need exists for an empirical theology that makes its concepts clear by reference to experienced events within the context of a candid pluralism and relativism. Hence, I call for a new modernism. A pragmatic, empirical approach leading to a form of naturalistic theism has much to offer in the current search for a theology that is both credible and useful. The roots of this outlook can be found in a group of American theologians who did their work in the first third of this century and who have long been forgotten by all but a few of us. Yet the fact is that some of the best thinking today is already closer to the modernist alternative than is generally recognized.[45]

Let me stress that my call is not for a simple reproduction of the old modernism of Shailer Mathews, Shirley Jackson Case, Henry Nelson Wieman, and others. The need is for a new modernism that shares some but not all of their methodological and theological assumptions. The content of a theology useful for today will be different. Chicago modernism in the 1920's was, in some ways, the last gasp of the Enlightenment. Their too unambiguous hope in the blessings science would bring and their too easy resolution of the threats and terrors of existence cannot be our stance. Freud, Marx, Nietzsche, and Kierkegaard must inform us so that we can get past the illusion that we have no illusions. They were more confident (or ambiguous) than we ought to be about whether truth or at least the means to secure it is achievable.

Neo-modernism must come through and not around neo-orthodoxy. The optimism about history and human possibilities some of the earlier modernists espoused must be rejected on empirical grounds -- their own standard. The tragedies and absurd evils of everyday common life, the threat of nuclear destruction and of ecological catastrophe, the poverty and injustices endured by the wretched masses of the earth, as well as the ambiguous character of history generally require a realism absent in the more sanguine outlook of Mathews. Essential, however, is a realistic hope that a better society is possible as human beings respond with justice-producing actions to the gift and promise of divine purpose ingredient in nature and life. For modernists old and new this hope must be grounded in the real potentials of actual history, not based on faith that God will, from the future, bring about *creatio ex nihilo* a perfected social order.[46]

No detailed interpretation of the assumptions and procedures of the Chicago modernists is needed here, but this essay agrees with them at least in the following particulars.[47] Shailer Mathews is my primary point of reference.

1. Religion, whatever else it may be, seeks to relate persons and groups salvifically to what they regard as ultimate in their cosmic environment.

2. Christianity is a social movement in general world history and of Western civilization. No special or supernatural assumptions are needed to explain its origin or development. Its center is the way, the truth, and the life incarnate in Jesus of Nazareth.

3. Doctrines interpret the religious experience of the Christian community and function pragmatically to serve the spiritual needs of people. Belief systems are relative to the socio-cultural setting in which they arise. They change as one "social mind" (Mathews -- a set of assumptions that define the mentality of an epoch) is succeeded by another.

4. Based on a study of the origin and development of the Christian movement in its socio-historical environment, the function of theology is to discover convincing and useful values within this history and to restate them in a conceptual system that is appropriate for the prevailing "social mind." Central to this way of understanding life are the methods and conclusions of the empirical sciences.

5. The Bible is neither the norm of universal truth, nor does it contain such a criterion. It is a valuable source of insight that provides continuity with the Christian past. The truth and value of its teachings, however, must be judged by its capacity to meet human needs as they are felt and understood today. Whatever in the Bible assists persons to relate redemptively to the Creative Cosmic Processes and to achieve fullness of life for all human beings is to be appropriated. What does not serve this function is regarded as either irrelevant or harmful and is to be rejected.

6. Doctrines of God are not literally true. Nevertheless, they define relations between persons and whatever created them. They are historically conditioned conceptual formulations that function pragmatically to facilitate saving relationships with the Ultimate Environment. God is the name for the creativity in the cosmos upon which human beings depend for their origin and destiny.

7. Modernism is primarily a stance and a method, although it includes a body of theological doctrines.

I propose a new modernism in the spirit of Shailer Mathews. Important are his assumptions regarding the relativity of Christianity and of the conceptual frameworks that support systems of theology in a given cultural epoch. Equally significant are his theistic naturalism, his empiricism, and his pragmatism. Doctrines are tested by their power to relate persons to God in salvific ways. In order to do so, they must be worthy of belief as measured by the convincing conceptual assumptions of the age. They must be relevant to felt needs and experiences of people in a given situation. As a pluralist and relativist, I can never be sure that what I take to be worthy of belief correctly describes what is objectively the case, i. e., corresponds to reality. It is not at all clear what correspondence between a belief and reality means beyond some pragmatic definition. If being a pragmatist means never having to say you are certain,[48] the modernist is at least relieved of that burden. All this, of course, must be determined by some interpreter, making pluralism inescapable.

With respect to the understanding of God, neo-modernism offers an empirically-grounded naturalistic theism. God is the Creative Purpose ingredient in life creating, life-promoting events. All theological terms and claims that speak of hope and salvation are grounded in some experience of value-potential, value-production, and value-increase here and now. The divine element is discovered in events concretely experienced. All theological claims are tested by what is going on in nature and history as known in experience. The evolutionary process is the mythically-understood story of the divine adventure elaborating an experimental history aimed at producing ever more complex organisms and maximizing their enjoyment. Along such lines theologies of hope and liberation can be produced that are more modest though rhetorically less dramatic than some popular alternatives getting more press. However, they will not be burdened with spectacular claims that only a leap of faith can embrace but that no present experience can either establish or refute. A pragmatic, empirical naturalistic theism can be plausibly regarded as a valid modernizing of biblical themes related to God's creation and redemption of the world. The modernist will not insist, however, that such a vision is a reproduction of some original model in which only the form and superficial details have been altered but not the substance. This game is not worth playing anymore, though it is still the most popular activity in Theology City.

Modernism can be challenged at two vulnerable points. (1) Its greatest danger is that it will surrender to the ruling fashions of the age and forget the deeper insight in its Christian past. The modernist replies that no fail-safe method exists to save either the orthodox from foolish devotion to the mistakes or anachronisms of the past or the modernists from being seduced by the novel enthusiasms of the present. (2) If credibility and saving potential as measured by persons and groups here and now are the final appeals, the Christian validity of a modernist outlook is jeopardized. Three points can be made in response. (a) Modernists feel deeply their rootedness in the Christian past. That identity matters but not ultimately. Salvation is the ultimate concern, not being Christian.[49] (b) They claim that what they preserve is not incidental or peripheral to the biblical witness but important and basic to it. They continue to work out their own theologies in deliberate conversation with the Bible and Christian tradition.

CONCLUSION

Neo-modernists take a stand in the present as selves in the world seeking a way of intelligent practice that is most conducive to the increase of human, non-human, and divine good. They are committed to preserving what is deemed worthy by contemporary standards from the historic tradition and from Scripture, not some assumed essence or permanent given, however defined. Nothing from the past is normative, not even an ensemble of "cultural-linguistic" rules (Lindbeck),[50] or an original community ethos (Schüssler Fiorenza). Moreover, modernists are dedicated to an outlook rooted in the Christian past because it is unsurpassed by anything presently available from any source and possibly unsurpassable in principle as a guide to life. The unity of Christianity is found in a religious-social movement consisting of people who have found the most compelling truth about life in the biblical witness. Modernists stand in that historic company. They continue to return to that ancient treasury because the clue to wisdom and the inspiration for living found there are superior to any yet discovered.

NOTES

1. Shailer Mathews defines modernism as "the use of the methods of modern science to find, state and use the permanent and central values of inherited orthodoxy in meeting the needs of a modern world." *The Faith of Modernism* (New York: The Macmillan Co., 1924), 23. The notion of permanent values may not be generally representative of the modernists. It stands in tension with the denial that neither Scripture nor tradition contains a normative essence that can be restated in modern dress. Yet Mathews and others did look for ways to connect themselves with the Christian past. Given their insistence that contemporary criteria must be used to judge the truth and value of all inherited traditions, a difficult question is posed with respect to preserving Christian identity. Mathews worked valiantly at this, sometimes speaking of "generic Christianity" as a core of affirmations that center around the saving influences springing from Jesus. At other times he sought for abiding patterns of thought that were expressed in a variety of changing categories produced by the succession of "social minds." See my essay "The Life and Thought of Shailer Mathews" in the introduction to Shailer Mathews, *Jesus on Social Institutions* (Philadelphia: Fortress Press, 1971), xxiv-xxxix.

2. See my *The Impact of American Religious Liberalism* (Washington: University Press of America, 1983).

3. Ibid., chapter 12. See also Gilkey, *Naming the Whirlwind* (Indianapolis: Bobbs-Merrill, 1970), 73-106.

4. Neo-liberal perhaps fits even better those who were closer to the older liberals, such as Daniel Day Williams (and other process theologians), John Bennett, and Robert Calhoun.

5. For a brief account of theology since 1960, along with references to the relevant literature, see my *Systematic Theology* (New York: The Edwin Mellen Press, 1986), 21-7, 411-42; see also, Langdon Gilkey, *Reaping the Whirlwind* (New York: The Seabury Press, 1981), 109-238.

6. See Gayraud Wilmore and James Cone (eds.), *Black Theology* (Maryknoll, NY: Orbis Books, 1979); Cone, *A Black Theology of Liberation* (Maryknoll, NY: Orbis Books, 1986).

7. See, for example, Jürgen Moltmann, *Theology of Hope* (New York: Harper & Row, 1967).

8. See John B. Cobb, Jr., *A Christian Natural Theology* (Philadelphia: Westminster Press, 1965), and Cobb and David Griffin, *Process Theology* (Philadelphia: Westminster Press, 1976).

9. The standard source here is David Tracy, *Blessed Rage for Order* (New York: Seabury Press, 1975).

10. David Tracy does not speak of recovering the "essence" of Christianity, but he does refer to the "meanings" found in the tradition or "the central motifs" or "central meanings" or "basic meanings." Ibid., 17, 34. This sounds pretty close to "essence."

11. Like so many contemporary efforts, David Tracy in *Pluralism and Ambiguity* (San Francisco: Harper & Row, 1987), succeeds better in describing the problem than in resolving it. Circles of interpretation overlap, and by being mutually open to transformation, we can enlarge our circles, but even the best success of "the analogical imagination" can never unite the centers of our interpretive circles at a single location.

12. The recent works of Gordon Kaufman are a good example of this. See his *In the Face of Mystery: A Constructive Theology* (Cambridge: Harvard University Press, 1993), *Theology and Imagination* (Philadelphia: Westminster Press, 1981), and *Theology for a Nuclear Age* (Philadelphia: Westminster Press, 1985). Sallie McFague's *Models of God* (Philadelphia: Fortress Press, 1987), and Rosemary Ruether's *Sexism and God-Talk* (Boston: Beacon Press, 1983), should probably be included here, as well as Elizabeth Schüssler Fiorenza's *In Memory of Her* (New York: Crossroad, 1984), and Carter Heyward's *The Redemption of God* (Washington: University Press of America, 1982).

13. The early Tracy stresses the universality of principles of right reason, while the later Tracy emphasizes the particularity represented in stubbornly conflicting traditions of thought. Others have noticed this too, including William Placher, *Unapologetic Theology* (Louisville: Westminster/John Knox Press, 1989), 154-9. In *Blessed Rage for Order*, he comes close to an old-fashioned natural theology in his claim that an appropriate transcendental or metaphysical philosophy can establish the necessary presuppositions of all thought and experience whatsoever. See 53-6, 146-171. Moreover, reason can point to signals of transcendence in experience that point to a divine dimension to reality. See 91-118. In *The Analogical Imagination* (New York: Crossroad, 1981), and *Plurality and Ambiguity* the historicity and relativity of thought are more prominent. Yet the denial of an absolute standpoint, as well as confidence that theology can stake out public claims, are present over the whole period. Only with great reluc-

tance, one surmises, does Tracy give up on the idea that right reasoning can lead us into the truth. Yes, but alas, when are we reasoning rightly about God? Who is doing it? We cannot be sure.

14. For a comparison of revisionist and post-liberal theologies, see Placher, *Unapologetic Theology*.

15. John B. Cobb, Jr., *Christ in a Pluralistic Age* (Philadelphia: The Westminster Press, 1975).

16. Typical feminist texts are Rosemary R. Ruether, *Sexism and God-Talk* (Boston: Beacon Press, 1983); Marjorie Suchocki, *God, Christ, Church* (New York: Crossroad, 1982); and Letty Russell, *Human Liberation in a Feminist Perspective* (Philadelphia: Westminster Press, 1974).

17. See Wilmore and Cone (eds.), *Black Theology*, 620-2, and Cone, *God of the Oppressed* (San Francisco: Harper & Row, 1975), 138-94.

18. James Cone, *A Black Theology of Liberation*, 35-9.

19. See *God of the Oppressed*, 16-107, and *A Black Theology of Liberation*, xxi-ii.

20. Cone can be read differently perhaps, i. e., as a thoroughgoing relativist, agnostic before the ultimate mysteries who confesses his own faith on the basis of undeniable conviction yet without being able to prove its objective truth. See *God of the Oppressed*, 102-7. That theme is present. Yet the philosophical skeptic is finally overcome by the Christian believer who cannot doubt that faith arises in a genuine encounter with a Living Word, an Other, a Liberating Subject, who calls the oppressed to claim their destiny as free subjects. The final, stronger theme is that faith grasps or is grasped by Reality, yielding not simply subjective confidence but objective truth. Or so I read him.

21. See *Gyn/Ecology* (Boston: Beacon Press, 1978).

22. Letha Scanzoni and Nancy Hardesty are evangelicals who state that "any teaching in regard to women must square with the basic theological thrust of the Bible." *All We're Meant to Be* (Waco: Word Books, 1974), 20. But they seem quite timid in saying that a given passage is just plain wrong rather than merely needing a contextual interpretation that makes it say something worthy. The resort to "the basic thrust of the Bible" as a norm opens a very wide door that allows the interpreter considerable latitude in defining acceptable biblical doctrine. The tension between appealing to specific texts, when good ones are available for our purposes, and resorting to "the basic thrust of the Bible," when they are not, poses a crucial methodological problem in both liberal and evangelical theologies.

23. *Sexism and God-Talk*, 12-46.

24. *In Memory of Her*, xiv-xxv, 1-95.

25. Ibid., 30-3.

26. Ibid., 105-59, 140-1.

27. It is of interest that Schüssler Fiorenza finds in Ruether (as well as in Letty Russell and Phyllis Trible) a neo-orthodox procedure of finding a canon within the canon, a universal essence of the Bible or Christian faith that can be distinguished from its time-bound form and accidental features. See *In Memory of Her*, 14-21. Her criticism of this procedure is telling: it abstracts from history an idealized pattern that is used to criticize the specific content of faith and practice and, in effect, to claim that the underlying essence of the tradition is different from its actual existence. But is that not that to play tricks with history? Unless Schüssler Fiorenza herself is saying merely that an egalitarian church actually existed and that women today can be empowered by identifying with and continuing that ancient minority tradition, then she is not entirely unfree from that tendency herself. I hear her saying that the discipleship of equals is not only fact, it is also normative for the Gospel by the Gospel's own internal standards.

28. Mary Daly, *Beyond God the Father* (Boston: Beacon Press, 1973), 73.

29. Numerous complex and subtle issues arise here. They might well claim that they did not invent the norm they employ but rather found it in the tradition and just recognize it as what is truly valid in it. Yet the tradition contains much else besides, which they reject. How is it that they make normative precisely what coincides with what a critical feminist principle requires? They can hardly claim that what they make normative in the tradition is what is explicitly normative in the Bible or the early church, since both admit that patriarchal and oppressive motifs are dominant. Certainly what is not dominant in the tradition can be made normative for us. Yet how can they claim that something not dominant in the tradition is definitive, not merely for us, but for the tradition itself? One might, of course, maintain that the implicit norm of the tradition itself really did require equality, mutuality, and universal justice but that the dominant interpretations of the community of faith failed to see that what they most deeply believed undermined the patriarchy they practiced. But that seems strained. Hence, while Ruether and Schüssler Fiorenza may have arrived at what they accept as normative as believers who have been informed by the Christian past, it would nevertheless appear that a modern critical feminist consciousness is the ultimate determinant, regardless of how they learned of or were convinced by the norms explicit and implicit in that consciousness. It is in that sense that I suggest that they accept only what is best in the tradition, whether or not it is dominant in or definitive for the tradition. They must forego any attempt to claim that what they take as normative for present-day believers simply *re*-presents what is self-defined

in the Bible as its essence. Even if Jesus himself turned out to be another patriarchal male, they would have to reject him too. That is the logic of the matter, although they are convinced that Jesus is on their side, or they are on his.

30. Sheila Greeve Davaney, "Problems with Feminist Theory: Historicity and the Search for Sure Foundations," in *Embodied Love*, ed. by Pauley M. Cooey, Sharon A. Farmer, and Mary Ellen Ross (San Francisco: Harper & Row, 1987), 79-95.

31. On one occasion, Bernard Loomer looked up after reading a sentence from the paper he was presenting and said, "As the Bible plainly teaches." He looked down, paused, looked up again, and said, "I don't know where, but it does." He looked back at his paper another time, paused, looked up once more, and concluded, "Well, if it doesn't, it ought to." Now there's a modernist after my own heart!

32. See Langdon Gilkey, *Reaping the Whirlwind*, 159-87.

33. See my *Systematic Theology*, 132-62.

34. Langdon Gilkey, "Cosmology, Ontology, and the Travail of Biblical Language," in *God's Activity in the World*, ed. by Owen Thomas (Chico, CA: Scholar's Press, 1983), 29-43.

35. For an excellent discussion of history and providence in modern Protestant theology, see Gilkey, *Reaping the Whirlwind*, 209-38.

36. See his *The Nature and Destiny of Man*, One vol. ed. (New York: Charles Scribner's Sons, 1949), II:287-301, and *Faith and History* (New York: Charles Scribner's Sons, 1949).

37. See, for example, David R. Griffin, *God, Power and Evil* (Philadelphia: Westminster Press, 1976), 251-310.

38. Schubert Ogden, *The Reality of God* (New York: Harper & Row, 1966).

39. Langdon Gilkey, *Reaping the Whirlwind*, 361n35.

40. "It is not clear, at least to this writer, whether Moltmann believes the promise will someday really be fulfilled, whether he thinks it may be fulfilled, or whether his concern is entirely for the meaning of life here and now in light of the promise, so that the question of its actual fulfillment in the future does not arise." John B. Cobb, Jr., *Process Theology as Political Theology* (Philadelphia: Westminster Press, 1982), 69. My reading of Moltmann is that he thinks the promise really will be fulfilled. See *Theology of Hope*, 15-22, 216-29, 288-91. Delwin Brown, *To Set at Liberty* (Maryknoll, NY: Orbis Books, 1981), 113-21, and Langdon Gilkey, *Reaping the Whirlwind*, 226-38, also read him as referring to an objective fulfillment, total and complete, on the very earth on which Christ was crucified. I agree with Cobb, however, that Moltmann is not always clear.

41. William R. Jones, *Is God a White Racist?* (Garden City : Doubleday, 1973). For Cone's response, see *God of the Oppressed*, 138-94.

42. Jürgen Moltmann, *Theology of Hope*, 288-91, 325-38.

43. See Thomas (ed.), *God's Activity in the World*.

44. Whiteheadian theologians will protest that their God does offer a particular providence for particular occasions. Yes, but this God only persuades, violates no general laws of nature, and guarantees no outcomes. The result is not an exception to providence viewed in terms of a general outworking of purpose in and through the whole network of finite events. Taken as a pragmatically useful philosophical myth and not as a metaphysical theory that purports to be literally true, Whitehead's vision is compelling. But he does not claim that God unilaterally accomplishes specific things, as the biblical and classical God clearly did.

45. The recent naturalistic theism of Gordon Kaufman interprets the reality of God in terms similar to those proposed by Shailer Mathews. Both connect God closely with the complex of natural forces that gave rise in the evolutionary process to human life. See Kaufman, *Theology for a Nuclear Age*, 30-46. But nowhere do I find any hint that Kaufman sees the connection. John Cobb, however, does get the Chicago school into the picture in his discussion of recent political theology. See *Process Theology as Political Theology*, 19-43.

46. Cf., for example, Jürgen Moltmann, *Theology of Hope*.

47. See my *The Impact of American Religious Liberalism*, 147-68, 188-206; my introduction to Mathews in the reprint I edited of *Jesus on Social Institutions*, xi-lxxii; Kenneth L. Smith, *Shailer Mathews: Theologian of Social Process* (Ph. D. Dissertation, Duke University, 1959); William J. Hynes, *Shirley Jackson Case and the Chicago School: The Socio-Historical Method* (Chico, CA: Scholars Press, 1981); and Creighton Peden, *The Chicago School: Voices in Liberal Religious Thought* (Bristol, IN: Wyndam Hall Press, 1987).

48. Jeffrey Stout, *Ethics after Babel* (Boston: Beacon Press, 1988), 297.

49. Here I differ from Paul Tillich. He says that a Christian is one for whom the content of the Christian circle is a matter of ultimate concern. I say that salvation is the ultimate concern. Being a Christian is the way to salvation. See Tillich, *Systematic Theology* (Chicago: University of Chicago Press, 1951), I:8-11.

50. George Lindbeck, *The Nature of Doctrine* (Philadelphia: The Westminster Press, 1984).

Chapter Two

The Authority of the Bible: A Modernist View

The Polish philosopher Leszek Kolakowski set forth the Law of the Infinite Cornucopia, which notes that no shortage exists of reasons to bolster whatever theory anyone wants to believe.[1] I suggest a theological version that I will call the Law of Infinite Hermeneutical Adaptability. This law states that the Bible can be interpreted so as to make it compatible with nearly every conceivable doctrine. The greatest proof of the operation of this Law is that irreconcilable positions on nearly every theological and ethical question are extant, all of which claim to have the sanction of Scripture. The sublime form of the Law indicates that reasons can always be given to demonstrate that Jesus himself would have approved of the conclusions reached by a given individual or community. When the Law of Infinite Hermeneutical Adaptability is in operation, it is nearly always accompanied by the Phenomenon of Total Surprise. I prefer the description of this Phenomenon in its "Lo and Behold" form: When individuals and groups find the Word of God in the Bible, the results, lo and behold, turn out to be identical with what they themselves believe!

The question I have repeatedly put to myself and to others in recent years is whether the Bible can be used with integrity. My answer is that it is possible and actually does occur. Nevertheless, joy is always warranted when it is observed. I have encouraged others to search with me for methods to increase the quality and frequency of probity in matters hermeneutical and exegetical. I have found my own way of being honest with Scripture by becoming a modernist. Perhaps my outlook would better be called neo-modernism, since I am addressing a situation quite different from that to which Christian modernism spoke seven decades ago.[2] Shailer Mathews is my Baptist and theological forefather, but I am not committed to everything he wrote during the first third of this century. His optimism about history is far too shallow for this more tormented age. His excessive reliance on science and his neglect of philosophy are weaknesses, to my mind. Yet his approach to the Bible, his understanding of Christianity as a religious-social movement, and his conception of theological method are worthy of re-examination.[3]

CHRISTIAN MODERNISM

Christian modernists initially take a stand not as believers belonging to the church but as selves existing in the world. They become Christians because that form of belief and practice offers the best hope of achieving the best life possible for themselves and others. Modernists employ only experience and reason to discover and evaluate truth. Typically, they are relativists and pluralists who recognize that it is their reason and their experience that are decisive. Hence, they do not make universal claims for their conclusions. Many modernists are also pragmatists whose final judgments about matters religious and ethical are made in terms of whether a given way of believing and behaving facilitates satisfactory coping with the challenges of living.

At they same time, they affirm as worthy of belief motifs central to the Bible because they contain permanent and indispensable value. What is precious in the Christian past must be reinterpreted in thoroughgoing fashion in order to rid tradition of what is awful and obsolete and in order to make the Gospel plausible to large numbers of modern persons. Twentieth-century modernism is primarily a method of approaching the Bible and Christian tradition. However, in its American Protestant versions it rejects elements fundamental to the orthodox vision of the Bible, God, and Jesus. Modernism also presents a critique of vague, inconsistent, and timid views of Scriptural authority found among present-day liberals. Some examples may be helpful.

ETHICS AND ESCHATOLOGY

Preachers, theologians, and exegetes who otherwise seem quite willing to make the words of Jesus an ultimate religious norm frequently find ways to qualify the eschatology of Matthew 25:31-46. How many fine sermons have we heard from liberal pulpits on the high ethical teachings urging service to the needy only to have verses 41 and 46 passed over as if they were not even there! Liberals, of course, generally do not believe in the everlasting punishment of the wicked. Can the ethics of Jesus in that passage be so totally separated from his eschatology? Historical critics may be able to persuade some that these are not the words of Jesus but an interpolation of the early church. The text itself puts this saying in the mouth of Jesus. Any reading to the contrary remains problematic. Besides, the doctrine is there, whatever the authorship.

MARRIAGE AND DIVORCE

Jesus' words about divorce have been the source of much unnecessary suffering and needless guilt when dogmatically and literally imposed as an absolute legal code (Matt. 5:31-32, 19:9; Mk. 10:2-12; Lk. 16:18). Some conservative interpreters who are willing to deliteralize some of the other "hard sayings" in the Sermon on the Mount (Matt. 5:38-42, e. g.) have turned legalist when reading Matt. 5:31-32. I grew up among Christians who followed that path. A person who felt the call to preach could be forgiven for most anything in his (descriptively correct!) past except divorce. I have heard converts on their way to ordination recite their sordid history before the Lord brought them to repentance, and the people rejoiced. But no pastoral call was issued to divorcees. Even as a child I never understood why this sin was almost unforgivable. Is any of the fault in the text itself? This passage, after all, reads like a specific obeyable law and not like an impractical absolute ideal.

Taking all three Gospels together, the teachings are: Divorce is contrary to the divine intention, and the marriage union is not to be broken for any reason (Mark and Luke), except when adultery has occurred (Matthew). Do the passages in Mark and Luke imply that divorce is never the best of available options under any circumstances? Surely that cannot be defended. Matthew allows divorce for men when the wife is guilty of adultery. Should not women have the same privilege if their husbands are unfaithful? Moreover, the idea that divorce may be allowed for adultery but not for constant cruelty, chronic neglect, and total abandonment and the like is morally indefensible in the light of the most realistic and compassionate perspective available to us.

Others, among them some liberals, have turned to textual analysis for help. Maybe the Matthean version (5:31-32, 19:1-12) that permits divorce only on grounds of adultery was an addition of the church. Another strategy is to suggest that maybe the Markan (10:2-12) and Lukan (16:18) versions state an absolute ideal, a goal, rather than a literal command, like the hard sayings in the Sermon on the Mount (Matt. 5:38-48). This has much to commend it, but whether this is what Jesus intended is impossible to know. Fortunately, common sense, pastoral compassion, and human sensitivity have often mercifully found ways around these troublesome passages. Is there any interpretation of these texts that does not do violence either to the texts or to the highest moral consciousness? It is certainly difficult to harmonize everything that Jesus said about marriage and divorce in Matthew, Mark, and Luke. For example, Matthew speaks of divorce for men only, while Mark mentions the possibility of a wife divorcing her husband. In addition, what are we to do with the notion that all divorced persons who remarry are to be regarded as adulterers? Does that not imply an ontology of sex and marriage that, to say the least, is problematic for modern people? Most of us today do not have as part of our intellectual equipment the assumption that the union of a man and a woman in marriage establishes a permanent metaphysical reality that divorce (legal and spiritual) cannot negate.

In dealing with the reported words of Jesus on marriage and divorce, exegetes face a formidable challenge. Even William Barclay is compelled to write in this connection, "It is now that we are face to face with one of the most real and most acute difficulties in the New Testament."[4] However, even here there is a way out, and Barclay finds it. (1) In Mark 10:11-12 Jesus is taking into account the fact that in Gentile law a woman could divorce her husband, whereas in the Matthean passage the Jewish law is the referent, in which a woman could not divorce her husband. (2) The Markan and Lukan versions in which no cause is sufficient to justify divorce give us the real Jesus and not Matthew, who allows divorce for a man because of adultery. (3) The teaching of Jesus in Mark and Luke, however, states an ideal and a principle, not a law. Thus, in the end Barclay resolves all the acknowledged difficulties to locate an interpretation that is true to Jesus and to a moral viewpoint he can affirm. The operative principle in Barclay appears to be that the words of Jesus are truth. Is Barclay then guided by that assumption to come up with an explanation that fits what we otherwise know or believe about Jesus, as well as Barclay's own idealism on the topic?

I do not disagree with his conclusions, i. e., that ideally marriage is a life-long union of husband and wife but that realistically sometimes divorce may be the better choice. Moreover, failures are to be dealt with greater sympathy and less condemnation. My only point is that his treatment illustrates the principle of hermeneutical adaptability, namely, that scholarship and exegesis combine to produce outcomes acceptable to the particular interpreter. The fact that other equally competent scholars and exegetes work with the same texts to produce a variety of contrary outcomes indicates the pronounced subjectivity of the hermeneutical enterprise. The objective content of the text enters into the determination of the outcome through the minds of the exegetes, of course, but the final and decisive factor is the interpretation, not the Bible. The interpreter is the functional arbiter of truth, however much Jesus or the Bible may be given credit for the normative doctrine that is affirmed by the exegete.

Moreover, are not other views equally plausible in light of the texts? For example, could not one agree that marriage is ideally permanent but that, since Jesus allowed it, divorce is permissible when adultery occurs, that being a special case? Or could not one take Jesus to mean that since marriage establishes an indissoluble ontological union, neither law nor practice can in fact bring about a divorce. It follows that anyone divorced by law is still married to the previous partner in reality and in the sight of God. Hence, the only way the partners can be free to remarry is to demonstrate that the requisite conditions that constitute marriage were not present, hence no real marriage ever occurred. In that case, an annulment might be ordered that recognizes that no divorce is required since no true marriage in the ontological sense existed. Which, if any, of these views were intended by Jesus cannot be determined with certainty. The texts do not interpret themselves. Some interpreter produces the final product that prevails in actual life.

Don't we all keep interpreting until we get the Scriptures, in so far as they contain the Word of God for today, to fit what we deeply believe or can live with? We do so usually on the basis of *something* in the Bible itself. I have heard a professed inerrantist make I Cor. 14:34 sound like an injunction for women to speak up any time they want! By situational interpretation and by determining the meaning of one text by reference to another, he deauthoritized that passage right before our very eyes![5] Some conservatives work hard to find some spiritual or medical lesson in the injunction not to boil a kid in its mother's milk (Deut. 14:21). The gift of performing hermeneutical miracles has been distributed among many doctrinal persuasions. The modernist suspects that the interpreter is the author of the outcome more than the text itself in these cases. Hence, when someone concludes, "Thus sayeth the Lord," the theological consciousness and moral sensitivity of the exegete are in actual fact the functional authority at work, regardless of the view of biblical inspiration held by the interpreter.

HOMOSEXUALITY

The permissibilility of faithful, loving relationships between persons of the same sex divides churches today. Some liberals who want to make the case for the legitimacy of homosexual love are trying to find biblical support for their views or at least to take the offense out of those passages that are used by conservatives to condemn gay sex as sinful.[6] In an article in *The Christian Century* John McNeill refers to recent scholarly works on the subject and concludes that "nowhere in Scripture is there a clear condemnation of a loving sexual relationship between two gay persons."[7] Perhaps this is sound exegetical reasoning, although Lev. 18:22 and 20:13 seem pretty plain. These verses may not specifically refer to loving, faithful sexual relationships as we would understand them today but rather to the improper mixing of roles and categories. In that ancient culture the role of the man was to penetrate not to be penetrated. Nevertheless, suppose there were two hundred verses scattered through the Bible, including the Old and New Testaments and explicit words of Jesus unmistakenly condemning any and all sexual relationships between gay men or between lesbian women, would that make it wrong? If there were four hundred verses that legitimize homosexual love, does that make it right? I answer "not necessarily" to both questions.

All attempts to get answers to the modern questions we ask of Scripture in this regard can at best yield only a limited degree of probability that can never be beyond dispute among competent scholars. Do we really know what various biblical writers or communities would have said about the kind of relationships among homosexuals for which McNeill seeks biblical approval or at least permission? Why should the morality of homosexual love be settled by the intent or content or context of the original texts rather than by theological reflection in which specific passages are measured by the highest ethical norms we know, having learned them from Scripture? At the same time it must be insisted that careful historical study and responsible translation and interpretation may be effective in showing how the prejudices of the past have themselves corrupted the meaning of the original texts. Devotion to the text can sometimes prevent misuse of the text and lead to interpretations that are not only more accurate but more humane.

While he does relativise particular passages of Scripture and insist that love is the only absolute moral norm, even a liberal like Norman Pittenger seems more anxious than necessary to deny that certain passages condemn homosexual practice.[8] Letha Scanzoni and Virginia R. Mollenkott are evangelical scholars who clearly conclude that loving, faithful homosexual relationships are proper, but they are quite cautious in dealing with the biblical texts.[9] I would prefer to say that it does not matter what particular passages on the subject of homosexuality say, if they are not in harmony with principles that facilitate justice and the highest possible fulfillment of persons in community. Yet I can see the pastoral relevance of showing the error or questionability of certain traditional interpretations of Scripture that are oppressive when one is dealing with a conservative gay Christian who is troubled by the fact the Bible seems to condemn homosexual practice. One must, however, be completely honest with the actual texts in doing so.

Today conservatives quote Leviticus against homosexuals as if these texts were the authoritative Word of God (Lev. 18:22, 20:13). It does not seem to embarrass them that they conveniently ignore numerous other precepts in surrounding verses and chapters that do not serve their immediate interests, but which, presumably, should be equally binding. How many raise objection to hybrid cattle (Lev. 19:19)? Do they feel guilty when wearing garments containing more than one kind of fabric (Deut.22:11)? Should they? Is it an abomination for women today to wear men's trousers (Deut. 22:5)? Would they also advocate that those caught engaging in homosexual acts should be put to death? The law of Leviticus does (20:13). Should heterosexuals who commit adultery be executed (Deut. 22:22)? Should fundamentalists allow women to teach an adult Sunday School class, some of whose members are men (I Tim. 2:12)? The text says women are to keep silent. In how many churches is this rule obeyed? Happily, it is generally ignored or creatively dismissed.

Are there any Christian exegetes, by the way, who personally believe that homosexual practice in loving fidelity is wrong but who do not think the Bible supports them on the issue? Or have the exegetes who, on textual grounds, try to weaken the biblical injunctions against it already decided on some compelling basis -- doubtless including *something* in Scripture itself -- that its prohibition is a cultural prejudice, not a moral truth? And is it not the case that conservatives who personally believe that homosexual sex is sinful find, lo and behold, that the Bible can be quoted to sanction their views. I do not accept the simple alternative view that liberals and conservatives assiduously study the Scriptures and then adopt as their own the views they find there that constitute the Bible speaking as the Word of God. It is much more complicated than that, even if exceptions can be found to my claims.

IS JESUS THE NORM?

Are the words and deeds of Jesus as such the norm? If so, then everything he said and did must be normative. It does take a little imagination and maybe even a little fudging to make the not-so-nice initial response of Jesus to the Canaanite woman look good (Matt. 15:21-28). William Barclay has the tone of voice and sweet smile of Jesus take the insult out of his calling her a dog. Besides he used the word for cute, little household pets and not the one for big, ugly garbage heap mongrels.[10] Or maybe he was just testing her faith, and, anyway, he healed her daughter didn't he? Jesus apparently approves the vicious killing of the tenants by a householder who had been wronged and suggests that God will be equally harsh with those who do not honor the divine son (Matt. 21:33-46). Some time ago I heard a sermon on this passage. When the preacher came to the end of the story, he skipped verse 41 altogether.

What hermeneutical principles should guide us in dealing with the words of Jesus? Are they -- all of them -- the very definition of the highest and best in Scripture? Or are they to be judged by the highest and best in Scripture, like all other passages in the Bible? The outlook of Jesus reflects a historically-conditioned outlook that requires interpretation in the light of the final revelation defined by his role as the Christ. Hence, not everything the historical Jesus said or did -- assuming we can know for sure what he did say -- is necessarily expressive of the unity of God in Christ. It is also true, however, that the words and deeds of Jesus are the data we use to define the normative Christ by which specific words and deeds of the historical Jesus are in a reverse movement concretely judged. By normative Christ I mean someone's interpretation of what it is in Jesus that constitutes truth about God and human existence. As a modernist I would further urge that everything in Scripture, including the words and deeds of Jesus, must be judged by the highest and best we know from all sources. As Christians we will acknowledge that the Bible and Jesus are chief among the sources from which we have learned what is most excellent in the way of religious belief and moral practice.

THE MODERNIST VIEW

The modernist view is that everything in Scripture must be judged by what is most excellent in its witness, and it is we the interpreters who decide that. *Agape* as the defining standard of God's character and actions and as the measure of human responsibility is not only the highest and best that is to be found in the Bible but is the normative guide to life here and now. I would urge that this form of love is the best that we know from all sources up to now. That is the reason it becomes our norm. Moreover, it is central to the New Testament vision of religion and morality. *Agape* seeks to meet the need and promote the good of the neighbor. *Agape* promotes justice for all and works to increase the well-being of all persons. It regards the neighbor as equal to oneself. Hence, homosexuality is to be judged by whether persons are damaged or edified by its practice, whether need is met and well-being is fostered, whether healthy and mutually supporting relationships are nurtured. The text of the New Testament is the indispensable source of the meaning of *agape*. Particular passages are relevant to the determination of its implications for morality but not necessarily determinative in specific instances. The apostolic witness to the requirements of the Christian life are historically and culturally conditioned, as are ours. Some interpreter has to make a judgment here and now about the matter *and* take responsibility for that judgment. This decision may differ from portions of the New Testament perspective. For example, Christians today must say something different about slavery, obedience to the state, and about women than do some passages in the canonical books.

This does not mean that careful and responsible exegesis is unimportant. Neither is the Bible dispensable once its zenith has been located. The whole of Christian belief is not to be reduced to a few central motifs stated in general terms, from which all else may be deduced here and now as the occasion arises. No advocacy is being made of theological act-situationalism, in which in every instance one appeals directly to abstracted normative principles unmediated through particular passages. Actually, that method might work out as well or better than a mere picking and choosing of passages that we like or happen to agree with and calling them authoritative. The biblical treasure is to be found nowhere else than in its own concrete and diverse witness.

The love of God for the world and the love of God and neighbor required of us is the norm by which all is to be measured when Christian doctrine is to be articulated. The norm itself is derived from the particular expressions of human witness that compose the Bible. Moreover, both Testaments are rich with profound explorations of the human predicament and the divine remedy. The Bible is filled with marvelous testimonies to the divine character and purpose as humanly experienced. It abounds in eloquent pointers to a fitting response to God's initiative in creating, governing, judging, and redeeming the world. The images, insights, ideas, and portrayals of God and humanity expressed in narrative, poetry, parable, Gospel proclamation, moral exhortation, and in all the other varieties of witness and reflection constitute a great treasure indeed. This gold can be mined only by arduous and detailed examination and responsible interpretation.

The modernist approach furnishes a way to use the Bible that is completely honest. It eliminates the need to find procedures to make sure that we can claim the authority of that ancient document for beliefs and values that we find compelling. Yet we can also honor the Bible for the treasure it does contain in its witness to the love God has for us and to the love that God requires that we practice toward one another. Above all, it bids us take responsibility for our views. Let it be said plainly, however, that nothing in the Bible is authoritative merely because it is in the Bible or because Jesus said it. Authority resides in the fact that the biblical witness evokes acceptance by our reason in the light of our experience and all the relevant evidence we can bring to bear from all sources. The final verification is in terms of the capacity of biblical teachings to function salvifically in everyday life, not whether Scripture or Jesus authorizes them. There are, of course, other ways of using the Bible with integrity, but the modernist practice works best for me.

Notes

1. *New York Review of Books* (January 11, 1996), 10. In dealing with the question as to whether the average American worker is better or worse off now than a couple of decades ago, Prof. Frank Levy of the Massachusetts Institute of Technology remarked that by carefully selecting the data and by skillfully interpreting the facts, it is possible "to `prove' just about any proposition you want." Steven Pearlstein, "Are We Better Off or Not?" *The Washington Post National Weekly Edition* (March 13-19, 1996), 6.

2. See my *The Impact of American Religious Liberalism* (New York: Harper & Row, 1962; reprinted, Washington: University Press of America, 1983), 26-37, 147-168, 188-206, for a description of modernistic liberalism in its earlier manifestation and for an account of two of its chief exponents -- Shailer Mathews and Henry Nelson Wieman, both members of the "Chicago school" of theology.

3. See my summary and evaluation of his thought in Shailer Mathews, *Jesus on Social Institutions*, ed. by Kenneth Cauthen (Philadelphia: Fortress 1971), xi-lxxiii.

4. William Barclay, *The Gospel of Matthew*, Rev. ed. (Philadelphia: The Westminster Press, 1975), II:201.

5. A young candidate professing the inerrancy of Scripture came before a committee. I inquired if he believed that women should keep silent in the churches (I Cor. 14: 34), since he believed that every word in the Bible was profitable for instruction. He answered in the negative and spent the next

few minutes in a dazzling display of contextual interpretations, comparing passages with each other, etc. until in the end it appeared that Paul was actually encouraging women to speak up anytime they wanted! Even for the inerrantists it seems the Bible can be made compatible with whatever doctrine they feel is essential to truth and good practice. No matter what it *says*, it only *means* what we know it has to.

6. See, for example, John J. McNeill, *The Church and the Homosexual* (Kansas City: Sheed Andrews and McMeel, 1976), 37-66; 4th ed. (Boston: Beacon Press, 1993), 36-66.

7. John J. McNeill, "Homosexuality: Challenging the Churches to Grow," *The Christian Century* (March 11, 1987), 242-6. McNeill refers to recent works by George Edwards, *Gay/Lesbian Liberation: A Biblical Perspective* (Philadelphia: Pilgrim Press, 1984), and Robin Scroggs, *The New Testament and Homosexuality (Philadelphia: Fortress Press, 1964)*). The literature on the Bible and homosexuality has grown considerably during the last decade. For a recent survey, see Daniel A. Helminiak, *What the Bible Really Says about Homosexuality* (San Francisco: Alamo Square Press, 1994).

8. See *Gay Lifestyles* (Los Angeles: The Universal Fellowship Press, 1977), 77-87.

9. See *Is the Homosexual My Neighbor?* (San Francisco: Harper & Row, 1978; rev. ed., 1994).

10. William Barclay, *The Gospel of Matthew*, II:120-2.

Chapter Three

Hermeneutics:
A Playful but Serious Contention

"I am not a scholar on this issue but one who is seeking clarity and understanding."[1]

Christians employ many methods of biblical interpretation and make use of a variety of procedures to relate biblical truth to what is otherwise known or believed. When all is done and said, however, only two hermeneutical principles have fundamental status:

PRINCIPLE 1

NO CHRISTIAN ALLOWS THE BIBLE TO TEACH AS THE AUTHORITATIVE WORD OF GOD WHAT IS KNOWN OR BELIEVED (FOR WHATEVER REASONS) TO BE EITHER UNTRUE OR IMMORAL.

Two illustrations will suffice. John Calvin was concerned lest some unwary reader draw wrong conclusions from some plain words of Scripture. Genesis 6:6 tells us that God was grieved by the great wickedness that had come to pass on earth and was sorry for having created humanity. One might conclude that God interacts with the world in time and history, has feelings, and undergoes change. Calvin, however, could not allow Scripture to teach this because it would conflict with the received doctrine of divine impassibility. Hence, these words in Genesis cannot mean what they appear to mean. We know, he says, that God "cannot repent or grieve but remains forever the same in happy repose."[2]

Calvin "knows" that the doctrine of impassibility is true. He, therefore, has to find an interpretation of this passage that will not contradict what he is otherwise certain of. It doesn't matter what the reasons were that led him to the "knowledge" that God is beyond change and hence not responsive in time to events on earth. The point is that he "knows" (believes strongly untroubled by doubt?) that God is immutable and impassible. Therefore, he cannot allow the Bible to teach as the authoritative Word of God something that for him is obviously false.

A few years ago I sat on a committee of my local Baptist association examining a young man who wanted to be ordained. In his theological paper, he announced his belief in Scriptural inerrancy. I remarked that he, of course, held that women should keep silent in the churches, I Corinthians 14:34. After all, St. Paul says that this precept holds "in all the churches of the saints" (I Cor. 14:33b RSV). For the next ten minutes -- a beautiful maneuver it was -- he tried to show us that the contrary doctrine was correct. When he had finished, one almost had the impression that the Apostle was urging women to talk as much as they wanted! Although the words of the inerrant Bible say clearly that women should not speak, he affirmed on the basis of contextual interpretation, other New Testament passages, and so on that they should. He "knew" in his heart that to impose the mandate of female silence was wrong. Hence, he could not, would not, allow the Bible to teach as the authoritative Word of God what was contrary to this conviction, no matter what the passage said. It does not matter what the grounds for his belief in the right of women to speak were. Doubtless something in the Bible itself was one basis. We make a lot today of Gal. 3:28, for example. The point is that he had the conception, and not even an inerrant Bible could shake him loose from it. God would not ask us to do what is wrong. Thus, I Cor. 14:34, occurring in an infallible book, which in its entirety and in all its parts is the Word of God, cannot mean what it plainly says.

While two instances cannot demonstrate the enunciated claim, one might ask for counter-examples. Are there cases in which what a given Christian takes to be the Word of God is regarded as either untrue or immoral? The theological reason is not hard to find. God is the source, measure, and author of truth and righteousness and therefore cannot be the teacher of falsehood and wickedness. I repeat: it does not matter how we come to have our certainties about what is false and immoral. As long as we have them, we cannot find the Bible binding upon our consciences regarding these matters, no matter what given texts say. This has to do with matters of cosmology and miracles as well as with points of theology and morals. Hence, a modern Christian convinced of Darwinian notions of evolution cannot find it necessary to take the creation stories in Genesis 1 and 2 literally. Yet Christians for eighteen hundred years had no problem in doing so. For Augustine the Genesis account of the origin of the world was part of the revealed Word of God. So were all the reports of supernatural occurrences in the Bible. For liberal 20th century Christians informed by modern science, the cosmology and (most?) miracles of the Bible are identified with anachronistic modes of thought and thereby deauthoritized.

PRINCIPLE 2

EVERY CHRISTIAN FINDS WHAT THE BIBLE TEACHES AS THE AUTHORITATIVE WORD OF GOD TO BE IDENTICAL OR CONGRUENT WITH WHAT IS KNOWN OR BELIEVED (FOR WHATEVER REASONS) TO BE TRUE AND RIGHT.

The second principle is, in one sense, the opposite side of the first. Yet it is more subtle, slippery, and difficult. The main point is that when the theological task has been completed, by whatever method, it turns out that what the Bible teaches as the authoritative Word of God is identical (or at least congruent) with the theology of the interpreter! This statement may appear to be a mere tautology, and a trivial one at that. It is less harmless, however, when the intended meaning is made explicit. The contention is that what the theologian, for whatever reasons, believes to be true about ultimate matters of faith and morals is proposed as the Word of God for today. The opposite claim will be preferred by many, namely, that one discovers the authentic Word from God contained in Scripture. **That** is what one believes to be true and right in matters theological and ethical. Well, yes, but what the Scripture teaches as the Word of God is always determined by some interpreter. Much more goes into every theology than anyone ever gets or could get out of the Bible. This "much more" sets the framework and limits within which the Bible can speak authoritatively at any given moment. The interpreter constructs the guiding principles and procedures by which given texts are explicated. As a consequence, no one ever hears in the words of the Bible a Word of God that contradicts what that person cannot doubt or is compelled to affirm as true, good, right, and beautiful. Instead, the truth one finds in Scripture turns out to be exactly what the interpreter believes.

The crucial question is, of course, located in the phrase "for whatever reasons." Obviously among the reasons Christians believe what they do is that the Bible teaches it, or at least they think it does. As Socrates said in *The Republic* as the true understanding of justice was about to be revealed, "I think we are in the vicinity of the treasure we seek." The Bible says many things. What it teaches as the authoritative Word of God (read religious and moral truth) is determined by some interpreter. And, lo and behold, what every interpreter discovers in the Bible when it speaks as the Word of God (bearer of normative theology and ethics) is identical with her/his own theology. This does not mean, let it be said plainly, that the theology is worked out independently of the Bible and then arbitrarily imposed. Doctrines are the result of an encounter of the Bible and an interpreter in a given cultural situation guided by some set of presuppositions. The content of the Bible, when regarded as regulative or normative in some sense, enters into the formation of the outcome. The crucial question has to do with how the terms that define that final product are set. They are always established by the interpreter. Interpretation is a constructive work of reason and imagination that takes place within shifting cultural modes of cultural and individual consciousness. On occasion, when the conditions are ripe for change, one's theology may be altered on the basis of a re-reading of the Scriptures. Novel circumstances sometimes enable us to see what was previously hidden or overlooked. The process of interpreting and reinterpreting is complex and not reducible to any simple formula. The Bible says what it says. It does not tell us how to interpret it or when it is interpreted properly.

The heart of the matter, however, can be put this way: *The text may have the first and third or second and fourth and the next to last word, but the interpreter has the intervening words and the last word. It is the last word that ultimately counts.* Who will adjudicate disputes between rival hermeneutical theories or claims about the meaning of revelation or the authority of the Bible or the impassibility of God or the role of women? Another interpreter will. On what basis? Some particular ensemble of theological and hermeneutical doctrines. From this chain of endless interpretations no escape can be found, only temporary resting places.

To use the terminology popular in many quarters today, interpretation involves a "fusion of horizons"[3] (Gadamer), the world of the text and the world of the interpreter. The decisive question, however, is what determines the way the fusion is to take place. The answer is that the fusion takes place in accordance with the rules and decisions of some interpreter. So this question resolves into another. *Who* determines how the fusion occurs and the results thereof? The answer is: an interpreter who practices some theory of interpretation. Which theory is right, best, proper, necessary, most useful? Mine, of course! No hermeneutical theory of any interpreter can deliver us from debates about hermeneutics. Every proposal takes its place among the rivals to be accepted or rejected by other interpreters.

What we need is metahermeneutics, a theory that tells us how rival hermeneutical theories are born. Why does interpreter A embrace interpretation theory B, while interpreter C is drawn to hermeneutics D? Alas, any metahermeneutical theory would generate rivals. The argument would get transferred to another level. No all-transcending supertheory can be formulated that can be used to grade all ordinary ones.

The most fascinating aspect of all this is to observe how interpretations of the Bible have changed. A century and a half ago scholars in the South, supported by many notable theologians in the North, found biblical support, or at least permission, for the practice of slavery. No one today who claimed that the Bible speaking as the Word of God justifies slavery would be taken seriously.[4] Why not? The Bible has not changed. The pro-slavery advocates could make a good case for their position based on what the Bible says and does not say. If the Bible has not changed, what has? Cultural consciousness has changed. Today we "know" slavery is wrong. Therefore, the Bible cannot be allowed, when it speaks as the authoritative Word of God binding on Christian belief and practice, to legitimize one person owning another, no matter what it says on the subject.

John Calvin interpreted biblical passages to make them fit the impassibility doctrine. Notions of a temporal, responsive, changing God are commonplace today. Theologians who believe that God is affected in some respects by interacting with the world have no difficulty finding biblical support for their ideas. Genesis 6:6 can be quoted in favor of thoughts Calvin rejected, even while admitting the mythological or symbolic character of the language involved. Notions of change, development, evolution, and of the importance of time are deeply rooted in modern modes of thinking. Hence, we are not scandalized by the possibility that God might change in some ways. This enables us to hear the Bible, speaking as the Word of God, teaching things about the Creator that classical traditions in theology found abhorrent. We can find a great deal in the biblical presentation of God's relation to time, history, and people to justify that conclusion. It looks to many of us as if Calvin -- and practically everybody else for centuries -- read the impassibility doctrine into the biblical framework rather than discovering it there.

The art of disposing of what is otherwise troublesome to a given scheme is well developed. The practice is well illustrated by classical theologians Augustine and Calvin, who both affirm a doctrine of limited election and yet harmonize this with I Timothy 2:4, which indicates that God "desires all men to be saved" (RSV). John Hick, a modern liberal, who believes in universal salvation, almost effortlessly stays in tune with the deepest intent of Scripture and of Jesus, who suggests a permanent separation of the righteous and the wicked (Matt. 25:31-46).[5] Fundamentalists and liberals alike have ways of dealing with Deuteronomy 21:18-21 that allow them to be "biblical" in their ethics without approving the stoning to death of stubbornly rebellious sons. No dishonesty is assumed in any of these parties.

In one sense, I am taking an obvious point and deliberately pushing it toward an untenable extreme. In my childhood among unsophisticated Bible-believing rural Baptists, a common saying was, "You can prove anything by the Bible." That was their common sense way of recognizing that the Bible could be interpreted in many ways, some of which conflicted with others. The usual procedure among Christians, including erudite scholars, is to go on from there to assume, either in practice or theory or both, that some interpretation is, of course, the right or better or at least the privileged one. We once-saved-always-saved Baptists "knew" that those possibility-of-falling-from-grace Methodists were just wrong. I intend to take the playfully exaggerated claim that anything can be proved by the Bible and ask what it implies for our hermeneutics as practiced, not as normatively described.

THE THREAT OF RELATIVISM

Does this throw us right into the middle of the dreaded sea of subjectivism and relativism? Of course it does, well, almost. Limits to interpretation do exist. The text does say just what it does say and not something else. The content of texts is a given that has to be dealt with. Moreover, with some relative success, a study of the

Bible as a whole reveals recurring themes, grand motifs, general patterns, ruling metaphors, and the like. The delineation of the biblical *Gestalt* produces a measure of agreement. Nevertheless, when thinkers set forth a normative theology, their appropriation of Scripture is mediated through a complex background of operative assumptions that determine the form and content of the outcome. The interpreter is the functional creator of the final product, however much the text of Scripture is a contributing source.

Hence, I affirm a more thoroughgoing relativism than most contemporary Christians. What is the alternative? The answer is that some position, usually ones own, is granted privileged status. For emphasis the voice may be raised, the desk pounded, and the foot stomped -- maneuvers that definitively settle the question. This may be done under the aegis of some theory of truth and objectivity that snatches victory from the jaws of relativism -- a triumph through fearless declaration. The bolder thinkers, of course, pronounce their opponents to be in error. The preferred conclusion, it is suggested, contains the authentic Gospel, if not in an unconditioned manner, at least in superior fashion to its rivals. Let anyone who doubts this consult a sample of contemporary theological writings. Over and over theologians claim, implicitly or explicitly, that their interpretation of what Scripture requires of us today in the way of belief and practice is closer to Jesus or the vital core of Scripture than contrary options, at least on the essentials. Is not such an avowal present in Walter Rauschenbusch, Karl Barth, James Cone, Elizabeth Schüssler Fiorenza, as well as in many others? Despite the threat of relativity, we all find ways to uncover the one universal Gospel, the real thing!

Paul Tillich recognized that various concrete norms have arisen over the centuries. Yet that did not deter him from also speaking of "the eternal message."[6] I wrote, before my most recent intellectual conversion, of the need for both a "universal" norm defining the single truth of the one and only Gospel and a "situational" norm that guarantees credibility and relevance for a specific context.[7] I was no more successful than Tillich or anyone else in saying how you can have conflicting perspectives that all teach the same "eternal message" identical with itself over the centuries.

It is not easy to locate universal truth in contrary concrete particulars, except in some highly formal and relatively empty propositions, such as God is one, Jesus is the Christ, or love your neighbor under all circumstances. These assertions are, of course, full of material content when compared to their alternatives -- God is many, Barabbas is the Christ, or hate your neighbor if she/he gets in your way. They are highly formal and relatively empty of content, however, when compared to the conflicting theologies that all share them in common. Hence, while they may define the boundaries of the playing field, they have comparatively little meaning useful for life unless spelled out in detail. For example, can you rightfully kill your neighbor under some circumstances? Here diversity, plurality, particularity, relativity, and disagreement galore enter. It is an old and difficult problem with no resolution that satisfies everyone.

Therefore, I am driven into an uncomfortable corner by questions like the following. How does it happen that what scholars in succeeding generations affirm Jesus to have taught about the Kingdom of God neatly coincides with the requirements of theological movements that rise and fall? Compare Adolf Harnack and Rudolf Bultmann. We have a chicken and egg question here. It could be that changes in New Testament interpretation lead to theological revolutions. I suspect that it works the other way around too. Mutual or coinciding origination from some underlying change in the larger society may occur. Alternating and reciprocal chains of influences, doubtless are also present sometimes. Can anyone doubt that deep underlying shifts in cultural consciousness in response to changing circumstances affect what we find the unchanging text of the Bible to be teaching as God's eternal Word for today? The immanent God of the 19th century liberals and the transcendent God of the 20th century neo-orthodox took turns being the real, the only, God that Jesus knew.

How does it happen that pacifists find the teachings of Jesus about non-resistance to evil binding, while adherents to the just war theory do not? The reason some Christians condemn all violence in pursuit of good causes while others condemn only some may be more fruitfully discovered by sociological, philosophical, and psychological inquiry than by looking at their exegetical conclusions, although that is important also. Differences in political outlook may be determined by social and historical location as well as by what Scriptural texts say. Theological conclusions may follow from cultural and experiential factors as well as from exegesis of Scripture. Why do Southern Baptists, who ordained me, make so much of Matt. 28:18-20 but much less of Matt. 25:31-46? Is the difference to be found in the texts or in the interpreters? Let it be said, however, that careful study of biblical texts may itself yield insights that shock, revolutionize, or otherwise transform the outlook of Christians with profound consequences. The context of the interpreter and of the text can, of course, be taken into account by exegetes of all persuasions. Yet no matter what exegesis reveals, it is we who exegete. We decide how we are to interpret the results as far as normative theology is concerned.

How can Christian feminists claim that the equality of the sexes expresses the vital core of biblical religion or the practice of Jesus, while traditionalists claim the same justification for the continued subordination of women? How are we to account for the different message from God that Calvin and present-day liberation theologians find in Scripture regarding the poor and wretched of the earth? The fact that Christians hold such diverse and contrary theological and moral views, all claiming the word they preach to be the Word of God (the truth), does not seem to create the doubts about the objectivity of the enterprise one would expect it might. Is it the Bible as such or a culturally, rationally, and experientially-produced perspective determining what in Scripture is God's Word to the church? Granted, the Bible is one of the sources of all these contrary outlooks in that *something* in it can be construed to have the proclaimed meaning. Yet it may be that the Bible has less to do with what Christians believe normatively about theological and moral questions than many professed views about Scriptural authority might indicate.

LIBERALS AND RELATIVISM

Some may protest that my polemic pertains mainly to fundamentalists and conservatives. I think not. Many liberals, meaning all non-conservatives of the 20th century, are no different in this respect. They, of course, acknowledge that the Bible is historically conditioned and culturally relative. They concede that all theologies are likewise historically relative and culturally conditioned. Yet in practice they pick and choose their Scripture references carefully to buttress their own moral and theological positions. They generally imply at least that their views are more biblical in some deeper sense than those of the fundamentalists, who may have about as good a claim as they, if we are to honor chapter and verse. One might expect that the recognition of relativity would lead them more often to say that this is the best they know up to now, that it is the only thing possible and workable taking everything into consideration from their point of view.

The customary principle for liberals is that if texts are available supporting their position, they quote them with the same fervor as do fundamentalists. If no passages can be found or if they teach an unacceptable doctrine, rescue is sought in more basic principles or motifs, or some overall biblical *Gestalt* -- what Nels Ferré once called, "the larger logic of the Bible." It is puzzling that while liberals acknowledge cultural relativity, in the end they over and again somehow manage to find the deepest and truest meaning of the Scriptures -- if not the one authentic Gospel itself -- in their own theologies! Liberation theologians are among the most recent of those who have played "at last we've got it."

Liberals may look askance on the mountaineers and rural folk who handle snakes and drink poisons as expressions of their piety. Is Mark 16:14-18 not in the New Testament? To the rejoinder that these verses were not part of the original manuscripts, one can simply say, "So what?" Does anyone seriously believe that their non-appearance in the earliest documents is the decisive reason why most Christians today do not fondle rattlesnakes or sip strychnine? Besides, even if the disputed verses in Mark were spoken by Jesus himself, some other reason could be found for deauthoritizing them as contemporary imperatives. Jesus did, after all, cast out demons. Moreover, he urged his disciples to do the same (Matt 10:8). Is exorcism in good odor among liberals? If Jesus' belief in demons is to be attributed to the relativity of Jesus' world view, then the door is open to relativise or reinterpret everything we think to be untrue or immoral. And, indeed, that door gets open so wide that we can get almost anything we want to through it. Oral Roberts has been subjected to much ridicule for reportedly claiming to have raised the dead. I doubt that he has done so. Nevertheless, what are we liberal Christians to do with Matt. 10:8? Why do we prefer to ignore that mandate to raise the dead but to make much of Matt. 25: 31-46? Even then we frequently hear only the ethical injunction, while ignoring the plain eschatological teaching that warns that those who do not serve human need will be cast into "the eternal fire" (RSV). Most liberals do not believe in a fiery hell after death. So is it not finally we who become the functional authority, not Jesus?

Of course, we must, liberals urge, distinguish between what is permanently valid in the New Testament witness to Jesus as the Christ and what is relative to that time and place. Yes, we must. That principle, however, grants authority to all sorts of doctrines. In particular, it makes it possible for us to assert that anything we do not believe but yet has textual support does not belong to the "essence." Somehow we manage to find our own favored doctrines very close to, if not definitive of, the vital core of what Jesus was all about. Yet we can hardly resist the conclusion that we discover what is somehow really there. No escape from relativity follows from locating the universal element in the person of Jesus or in the Christ, the incarnate Logos, and not in propositional descriptions. Jesus, the Logos, and the Christ remain relatively empty ciphers, void of much instruction for belief and action, as long as they remain uninterpreted. Every interpretation that spells out implications in sufficient enough detail to be a practical guide to life today will be as relative as the last one or the next one. Jesus has been claimed exclusively to authorize capitalism by some and socialism by others with equal certainty.

Recently in a regional newsletter of one of our more sophisticated communions, reference was made to the long tradition of healing in the church. An aside, gratuitously inserted, noted that some contemporaries like Ernest Angley make a "parody" of healing. Is there not at least as much biblical warrant for what the TV healer does as for what the author went on to describe as the ministry of two pastoral counselors? The implication was that Angley's work was not true to biblical tradition, while that of the pastoral counselors was. Should we laugh or cry at this? Counseling may attempt to cast out demons in some non-trivial sense and thus amount to an approximate equivalent for our time. Why should Brother Angley be thought of as engaging in travesty because he attempts to do the real thing, the same thing his Lord practiced and urged upon his disciples? Are liberals, by and large, any less modest than fundamentalists in claiming to lay hold on authentic biblical truth, despite their provisional recognition of relativism?

The claim that something is biblical, whether by today's fundamentalists or liberals or yesterday's orthodox Catholics and Protestants, means not much more than that some passage, principle, model, metaphor, symbolic core, or defining narrative or something can be found somewhere to ground the belief or practice in question. Little that has ever been approved by Christians, including persecution of heretics and slavery as well as the ministry of Martin Luther King, Jr., has lacked alleged biblical support. Limits there surely are to what can plausibly be supported theologically and ethically by the Bible. It would be fun on the basis of Christian history to try to say what they are.

THE MODERNIST VIEW

The modernist view contends that we decide what the Word of God is for us today. We have to. There is no alternative. We do anyway, even if we are trying honestly to discover or re-present some modern equivalent of what is objectively there. I propose that we stop claiming that the Bible is uniquely or decisively our warrant when we speak normatively and admit that it is our views that we are contending for. Why don't we say that the Bible is in the background as an influence or source? Why don't we frankly say that we regard as obligatory for today only what in Scripture is worthy of belief as we judge truth and right instructed by Scripture as we interpret it? It is finally the intrinsic excellence of what is professed and practiced that matters. We decide what that is.

The main objection to my recommendation is that it risks loss of Christian identity, maybe even abandons that aim entirely. My preliminary response is that even those who intend to preserve continuity with the Apostles cannot agree on what is necessary to the achievement of that objective or even on the criteria by which we are to judge the matter. Moreover, while the Gospel is contained in or witnessed to by Scripture, no one has been able to provide a concrete definition of the Gospel that satisfies all. Even if the Word of God is identified with Jesus Christ himself and not propositions of doctrine, no one can say what that means or implies for contemporary belief and practice in terms uninfected with particularity and relativity. *That* the Bible contains the Christian message is one thing. To say in words *what* is essential to its elucidation is another. The search for some universal essence, some vital core of belief, some ensemble of "cultural-linguistic" rules (George Lindbeck), or whatever, however defined, that is constitutive of Christian identity, is futile. But tomorrow somebody else will be trying and the following day refuted.

In the spirit of Shailer Mathews,[8] let us locate unity and continuity in the religious-social history of those persons and communities who have found truth and salvation in conversation with the biblical witness to God as known in the history of Israel and in Jesus functioning as the Christ. As Christians interpret this vision of life, they will divide themselves into groups and subgroups, sharing much in common but with theologies marked by particularity and relativity. The reason we continue to seek saving truth in the Bible is that it gives testimony to a way of living, believing, and hoping that is supremely if not unsurpassably excellent, as we judge the matter. Hence, while only what we take to be the highest and best in the Bible is to be preserved and re-presented in forms of thought credible to 20th century persons, it is in that ancient witness and in no other that the clue to wisdom with the power to save is empirically found. That too is one more interpretation.

Modernists recognize that their approach to the Bible and tradition raises serious questions about Christian identity. I too resist the notion that Christianity is merely whatever it has become wherever it appears. What is the alternative, given the fact that Christians cannot agree on what is essential to identity except in some very general or formal way empty of much specific content? History is filled with division and controversy on the essentials as well as on the details. Unity and identity are not problems only for modernists. Any definition of the heart of the faith must be provided by some interpreter. But which interpreter are we to trust with this important task? The fact is that those who claim to be Christians will continue to do so and will not submit to some authority who seeks to rule them in or out. All we can do is contend for our own versions of the faith as responsibly as we can with our minds and with our lives and live with the embarassment that some identify Christ with what we find abhorrent. In the last analysis the main departure of modernists from liberal Christians is that they see little profit in arguing about the form and content of a universal something that constitutes the one and only essential Gospel of Jesus and the Apostles. Also, they more self-consciously identify themselves as modern persons seeking fulfillment of life and are Christians for that reason.

In short, whether we affirm only what we take to be the best in Scripture (the modernist way) or the vital core that defines the universal Gospel (the liberal way) or some determinative set of "cultural-linguistic" prescriptions (the post-liberal way) or the full doctrinal content of an inerrant Bible (the fundamentalist way), or whatever, **we** decide which way we follow and what that choice implies. For all such judgments only relative validity can be claimed.

Unlike the student whose statement I quoted at the beginning of this chapter, I aspire to be a scholar on this issue. Like the student I also seek clarity and understanding. The modernist approach to Scripture has provided that for me.

NOTES

1. Student term paper, Fall, 1995.
2. Quoted in J. K. Mozley, *The Impassibility of God* (Cambridge: Cambridge University Press, 1926), 120.
3. Hans-Georg Gadamer, *Truth and Method*, 2nd ed. (New York: Continuum Publishing Co., 1995), 302-7, 374.
4. Alas, however, a few do even today claim God's approval for the practice. A state senator running for Congress in Alabama argued in May, 1996, that slavery is justified by the Bible and was good for African Americans. He quoted Lev. 25:44-46. My only consolation is that he is a Republican! Reported in *Democrat and Chronicle*, Rochester, NY (May 10, 1996), 19A.
5. John Hick, *Evil and the God of Love*, rev. ed. (San Francisco: Harper & Row, 1978), 346. Part of the problem hinges on what the Aramaic word meant that Jesus may have used for what is translated in English as eternal or everlasting in verses 41 and 46. My understanding is that the word in the text we have at least suggests that the damned will be there for a very long time, if not forever. The picture of the wicked in Gehenna in flames is conventional for the time, but in any case it is hard to get the universalism of Hick out of this text or any other specific words Jesus is reported to have spoken.
6. Paul Tillich, *Systematic Theology* (Chicago: University of Chicago Press, 1951), I:3-6, 47-52.
7. Kenneth Cauthen, *Systematic Theology: A Modern Protestant Approach* (Lewiston: The Edwin Mellen Press, 1986), 49-55.
8. For a summary of his views, see my introduction to his thought in Shailer Mathews, *Jesus on Social Institutions*, ed. by Kenneth Cauthen (Philadelphia: Fortress Press., 1971), xi-lxxiii.

Chapter Four

Seeing Through a Glass Darkly: A Modernist Credo for Today[1]

Robert Nozick says that a philosopher hopes to present arguments so powerful that they set up reverberations in your brain. If you reject the arguments, you die. Let me assure you that my aims are more modest and harmless. As we professionals say technically, I want to "share" with you some convictions about what being liberal might mean in the current generation. Already I have used the dreaded "L" word favorably. That appreciative mode will be sustained throughout.

I had hoped to got some help from John Cage, the composer and philosopher. In preparing for his recent Norton Lectures at Harvard, Cage compiled a list of 487 quotations from the great thinkers and from leading newspapers. He put them all into a computer and had

---

[1] This chapter was published in *Encounter* (Autumn, 1990), 377-88. Used by permission.

them split up and put back together randomly using a program based on the *I Ching*. Then he took out the words he didn't like, and that was his lecture. This procedure resulted in sayings like, "If there isn't any dust, why are you always taking baths?"

I decided to try this method. So I put together 487 quotations from the great theologians with some excerpts from *The New York Times*. I put them all in a computer and had them mixed up and recombined using a program designed to summarize the first 100,000 pages of Karl Barth's *Church Dogmatics* in a paragraph. Then I took out all the words I didn't like. And I thought I had my lecture. However, when I examined it, I found sentences like this:

"If there is no God, why is there so much suffering in the world?"

"If miracles really happen, could Jonah have swallowed the whale?"

"If Mary remained a virgin, why is Joseph smiling?"

At that point, I decided this method was not going to work! So I went back to my computer and started over.

THE BIBLE AND BELIEF

After considering a variety of topics that might go into a credo for liberals, I decided to restrict my attention to the first part of the creed that begins, "I believe." In particular, in what way is the Bible a source and norm of belief? Everything else we teach and preach depends on how we deal with the authority question. When I was in college I came across a book by Harry Emerson Fosdick that was immensely helpful to me when I was undergoing my first theological conversion. I use the title of that book for my topic: *The Modern Use of the Bible*. Fosdick was a Baptist reared in a religious environment similar to mine. He was dealing with questions I was asking as I learned about science, evolution, higher criticism of the Bible, and a whole range of post-Enlightenment developments. I became a liberal before I learned much about neo-orthodoxy. A few years later I wrote on theological liberalism for my doctoral thesis. Surprisingly, no volume on the subject was then in print. That dissertation became my first book. After a quarter of a century of first speaking the language of neo-orthodoxy and later taking up with a renegade band of process theologians, I have more recently become interested in the Chicago modernists of the 1920's and 30's, especially Shailer Mathews. So I come by my liberal credentials honestly.

WHAT IS LIBERALISM?

What is liberalism? Harry Emerson Fosdick always had the right phrase for the occasion. He said once that he wanted to be "a serious Christian and an intelligent modern." One could hardly express the aim of liberal Christians any better. *A liberal is a serious Christian who believes that the inherited faith has to be thoroughly reconstructed to be credible to intelligent moderns.* Fosdick described the liberals of his generation as standing between the fundamentalists on the right and the humanists on the left. The fundamentalists, he said, thought that if you changed astronomies, the stars would be lost. The humanists had concluded that there were no stars and never had been. Liberals believed that the stars were still there, just as they always were, but astronomies must change as knowledge advances. Abiding stars, changing astronomies. In religion that meant for Fosdick abiding experiences of God understood in changing categories of human thought.

Behind the liberal movement in theology was the discovery of the historical nature of reality, perhaps the most important intellectual legacy of the 19th century. The universe has come to its present state through a long process of development, passing through many stages along the way. Nature evolves, said Darwin. Human societies and human thought unfold over time, said Marx and Hegel. Even God has a history, said Whitehead. The consequences of thinking of reality in historical terms are enormous. History produces a variety of specific patterns of thought that come to be and pass away. Two fundamental assumptions follow that are crucial for theology. (1) All social and conceptual systems are human constructions that are historically relative and culturally conditioned. (2) A wide gap exists between the world view of the Bible and that of the modern world. This poses a difficult problem for theology. How can a Bible written in historically relative language provide an absolute revelation of God?

Liberals believe that the only way you can be a Christian is to make some sort of distinction between stars in the heavens (the everlasting Gospel) and the astronomies on earth that describe them (particular culture-bound theologies). The cosmology of Genesis, the ritual procedures of Leviticus, and the code of household duties in Ephesians do not belong to the universal Gospel. The effort to identify the abiding elements in Scripture took many forms. Some sought for the vital core or essence that transcends all cultures, enabling it to speak to every historical situation when translated into the appropriate thought forms. Some looked for the existential meaning found in biblical mythology. Others looked for the major motifs of the Bible as a whole and so on.

This procedure made it possible to have historical relativity and a Gospel for all times and places. The essential content remains the same although expressed in a variety of languages and conceptual schemes. What would otherwise be incredible or morally embarrassing could now be relegated to the historically conditioned vessel that contains the everlasting Gospel. Much effort during the last 150 years has gone into the search for this universal something that constitutes the abiding stars as distinct from changing astronomies. Endless unresolved arguments were predictably forthcoming. Unfortunately, while there was agreement that *something* is of permanent significance, no one was able to say *what* it was that commanded universal assent.

Nevertheless, this way of retrieving the Gospel made it possible for liberals to be "serious Christians and intelligent moderns." I use liberal in this connection in a broad sense to mean non-conservative or non-orthodox. Included are the evangelical liberals earlier in the century, a wide range of neo-orthodox thinkers, and a variety of feminist, black, liberation, and process theologians on the current scene. In this usage Walter Rauschenbusch, Reinhold Niebuhr, James Cone, and Rosemary Ruether are all liberals. For all of them, something contained in the Bible is the clue to the universal Gospel. Everything else in Scripture is measured by that. The older liberals typically found this vital core in the synoptic Jesus as a particular historical figure. Neo-orthodox theologians referred to the Christ-event as the normative Word of God. For Fosdick himself, the heart of Christianity is "reverence for personality." For Reinhold Niebuhr, it is a set of themes he called "biblical faith." For John Cobb, it is "the principle and process of creative transformation disclosed in Jesus as the Logos." For Ruether, it is the "prophetic-liberating tradition" that speaks of justice for the oppressed and of equality for male and female.

THE MODERNIST THESIS

I believe that the reconstruction of theology today must take a different approach. Systematic theologians like to make distinctions, and I must make one now. We can distinguish two ways of retrieving from Scripture what is authoritative for today. 1. One strategy is to locate something that defines the Bible's own religious vision that can be restated in categories appropriate for a given cultural situation. This I will call liberalism or the moderate way. It is the outlook of Walter Rauschenbusch, Harry Emerson Fosdick, Reinhold Niebuhr, Paul Tillich, James Cone, and George Lindbeck, to mention a few. 2. The other method is to claim for today only what is most excellent in the original Christian witness as judged by contemporary Christians. This I will call modernism or the radical way. It is the path followed by Shailer Mathews, Henry Nelson Wieman, Gordon Kaufman, Sallie McFague, and others. John Cobb, Rosemary Ruether, and Elizabeth Schlüssler Fiorenza operate much like modernists, but they claim to be discovering the one and only true Gospel. Theologians like to classify, but they do not like to be classified. Some will claim that they rise above my puny little taxonomy. How dare I categorize them anyway? They are just telling the truth! Let us grant that the line between the two ways is unclear in some theological writings.

I propose to take the more radical stance of the modernists. Let us give up the notion of an identifiable something that specifies what the one and only Gospel really and truly is. The appeal should be to the highest and best in Scripture given our particular standpoint as modern people informed both by Christian tradition and secular culture.

Two clarifying comments are necessary at once. (1) The highest and best of Scripture is authoritative because it is compelling as a way of believing and living -- and *only* for that reason. It is the most persuasive vision of life available to us in the world's inventory of religious possibilities. That is why we are committed to it. That is what makes us Christians. (2) We must take responsibility for deciding what in Scripture is worthy of belief today. All such judgments are relative to our own social location, interests, needs, life-history, and general outlook on things.

We do not often put it this way, but notice that the moderate way has a point of identity with fundamentalism. The fundamentalists appeal to an infallible, absolute Bible located in the original manuscripts. The older evangelical liberals gave that up but found a religious absolute in the historical Jesus. The neo-orthodox theologians also abandoned the infallible Bible but replaced it with a universal Christ-event. What will a contemporary modernist say to this? The difficulty with identifying something absolute, universal, and culture-transcending is that once we try to say exactly what it is, we reintroduce the very relativity, particularity, and culture-boundedness we were trying to escape. Neither the historical Jesus nor the Christ-event is accessible to us as an uninterpreted reality in itself. It is well and good to point to the historical Jesus or to the incarnation of God in Christ and say, "There, right there, teaching and healing by the Sea of Galilee or there on the cross, that's what I mean; there is the Word of God in flesh and deed." Nevertheless, to interpret what that Word means, says, and requires of us can only be done using human words that reflect some background theological theory.

Nevertheless, the search for something objective and reliable beyond the feeble, shifting opinions of theologians tossed to and fro by many winds of doctrine is extremely important. Undergirding this quest are two fundamental convictions: (1) The Christian Gospel is something definite that appeared in human history. It is what it is. It has its own identity. (2) Whatever the Christian message it, it is specified by the biblical witness to Jesus as the

Christ. If you want to find the Gospel, look in the Bible. Pointing to Jesus rather than to Socrates or Buddha or Marx identifies us as Christians. Unfortunately, the human predicament is such that once we get specific about what it is that is real, concretely defined, and located right there in Scripture, we can only provide a particular, historically relative account that is one among many. *That* the Christian vision is a historical reality objective to us and located in Scripture is true enough. Nevertheless, every attempt to say in human language what it normatively is introduces somebody's theological theory for which only relative validity can be claimed.

We deal here with a subtle but crucial point. Many liberals acknowledge relativity and plurality in all the ways I am contending for. Yet when they construct their own versions of the Gospel, they often appear to be claiming that their version is not just better for some purposes as they see it but better as an interpretation of the Gospel, truer to the original one and only real thing, the genuine article objectively considered. Now maybe what seems to be theological *hubris*, thinking of a theology more highly than one ought to think, is just outward exuberance that obscures inward humility. Their books often give a different impression. Often both things are being said: "My theology is just one more feeble attempt, destined to pass away." And, "I have seen more deeply into the one and only true Gospel than those who disagree." The result is a subtle ambiguity that needs to be exposed. The modernist is determined to say one thing: "My theology expresses the best vision of life, its predicament, and its possibilities that I have been able to find so far, and its roots are in Scripture."

Today we should acknowledge pluralism and relativism more radically than have most liberals. We must take our own finiteness and historical particularity with full seriousness. It is hard to resist the temptation to play "at last, we've got it." Now we know what that elusive essence is. Now we have discovered what the *real* Gospel is, maybe for the very first time since Jesus left the earth. It is, of course, defined in my theology better than it is in yours. *My Gospel* is identical with *the Gospel* or at least closer to it than yours -- that appears to be the message. Haven't we learned by now that any attempt to state what *the Gospel* uniquely and objectively is tells us as much about the interpreter as it does about the Gospel? The only alternative I know to the pluralism and relativism I advocate is to claim a privileged status for some contemporary way of believing that, despite all, is the real truth, *the* Gospel that Jesus himself taught and lived, or at least better than the alternatives.

THE INTERPRETER AS FUNCTIONAL AUTHORITY

So far the moderates might agree, although made a bit nervous by the direction things are going. The modernist, however, draws a further implication that may mark the parting of the ways more clearly. *The pragmatic, relativist, pluralist modernist goes on to say that functionally we become the authorities when we get down to specific cases of doctrines and morals.* The Bible says a lot of things, but it means little for what we are to believe and do today until somebody interprets it. Once that happens, we have one more particular, historically relative theology. We should acknowledge that and quit claiming some identity between our outlook and biblical truth as such. I suggest that everyone obeys the following hermeneutical rule: No one allows the Bible to teach as the authoritative Word of God for today what is strongly believed (for whatever reasons) to be either untrue or immoral. Hence, the modernist abandons the attempt to define in particular terms what the essence of the Gospel is, what true biblical faith is. It is not at all clear that there is any such thing as an objectively existing vital core of Scripture that is like a human face supposedly inside in a huge chunk of granite waiting to be chiseled out. At any rate, recovering it is conceptually impossible for history-bound creatures. Since we cannot agree on what it is, it is not much help to us merely to know that it is really there.

THE MODERNIST STANCE

At this point, the modernist goes one step further that may leave the moderate brothers and sisters in shock. The modernist has a self-conscious identity as a contemporary person in search of truth about life and the way to salvation. It is only because the Gospel presents itself as the best available candidate for the role of truth-telling about human existence and its possibilities that it is of existential interest anyway. Put most pointedly, the modernist is not primarily interested in the truth or essence of Christianity but in the truth about life. The Christian tradition is of concern because of its power to illuminate the meaning of this human pilgrimage as that can be judged by our own reason and experience here and now. The modernist is a Christian because the highest and best that can be found in the biblical witness is the most compelling vision of the reality of God, the meaning of life, and the way of salvation available. In Scripture is found the way, the truth, and the life. However, we appropriate from the Christian past only what is true and relevant to the increase of value in human and non-human life as we are able to judge that. What is crucial for us today is whatever it is, wherever it can be found, that can lead us to truth and to fullness of life. Modernist Christians find exactly that in the highest and best of Scripture. The vision of God and salvation found in the Bible is not only supremely excellent, but it appears to be unsurpassably good.

I believe this is the position to which a candid recognition of the relativity of knowledge leads us. We see through a glass darkly as creatures shaped by the time, place, and circumstances of our lives. Does this not leave us without a firm foundation on which to stand as we contend against the principalities and powers of darkness? No, I think not. Seeing through a glass darkly does not mean that we cannot see at all. It does mean that we need to move back and forth between two modes of life that should not be confused with each other. In one moment we will be passionately committed to what we presently believe to be true, right, and good. We will fight for it in all appropriate ways. In the other moment we will engage in disinterested reflection in which we will genuinely open ourselves to the possibility that a greater and deeper truth waits to be found. We will subject all our beliefs to questioning and earnestly seek to find the better way. When the time comes to do something, however, we will act in the sincere conviction that the best we know up to now is the truth that will make us free. When the time to testify comes, we will give witness to what we are compelled to believe and argue for what we cannot deny with all our might, cross my heart and hope to die. I call this alternation between passionate commitment and detached reflection living by the warm heart and the cool head. We need to avoid the religion of the cold heart and the baked brain.

SUMMARY OF THE ARGUMENT

It may help if I summarize this entangled argument. Then I want to illustrate the thesis. In order to deal with their recognition of historical relativity, liberals found it necessary to identify something universal in Scripture that could be distinguished from the particular world view in which it was expressed. The intent was to locate a Gospel that transcended all cultures that could speak to every culture. However, every attempt to express the unique faith once delivered to the saints turns out to be particular and relative, one interpretation among many. Each version differs from and sometimes conflicts with the others. Hence, plurality and relativity seem to undercut the original project of preserving the one and only true Gospel. Here enters the modernist, who makes a bold move. The modernist is a relativist and a pragmatist who centers on the importance of the interpreter. Every interpretation of biblical religion reflects the interests, needs, intellectual outlook, and cultural particularity of the interpreter. Relativism is not total, but it cannot be totally escaped either. In this situation, let us acknowledge pragmatically the priority of the interpreter and make the best of it. The most daring and dangerous move of the modernist is to insist that what is crucial is not the preservation of some ancient tradition but the achievement of salvation here and now. We must decide in the light of the best understanding we can come up with from any source what is most likely to save us if we act on it. The modernist Christian finds that saving truth in the Bible. The theological aim, however, is not to make a futile attempt to discover some universal, absolute definition of the one and only Gospel but to find some local and presently compelling interpretation that provides us with our best hope for now. That, however, is enough. It must be, since the alternative is fruitless. The modernist refuses to play, "at last, we've got it" -- always the most popular sport in Theology City.

The liberal says, "I seek the true essence of the objective Gospel, its real inmost meaning." The modernist says, "Don't worry about essence and universal truth. You can't capture it anyway. Just look for what is worth believing today. Besides, you liberals frequently reject no less and affirm no more than we do. When you come across something in the Bible you don't like, you just deny that it belongs to the essence. We modernists don't play that game anymore. The crucial question is whether something is worthy of belief, not whether there are biblical texts that either support it or reject it. It happens that the highest and best we modernists know, we trace to Scripture. It is either there explicitly, or it is suggested by something that is. We modernists take full responsibility for what we believe. Most of all, we do not try to overcome our relativity by claiming that *our Gospel* is *the Gospel*. Liberals sometimes sound as if they do make that identity. If you liberals say you don't, maybe you are one of us and need to come out in the open."

When we fight with one another over doctrines and morals, let us, then, candidly abandon the notion that the controversy is about who has correctly grasped the eternal verities found in Jesus or in Scripture. Let us simply bring the deepest insight we can find to bear on every challenge that arises. Our confession as Christians is that the vision we live by comes from the Bible as we interpret it.

CONTEMPORARY ILLUSTRATIONS OF THE THESIS

Let me give some examples of what this might mean on the contemporary scene. Some feminists insist that the vital heart and center of the biblical Gospel is equalitarian, despite all the texts in the Bible to the contrary. Some liberation theologians teach that the true Gospel is that God will emancipate the poor and oppressed on earth in some future yet to come, despite the fact that the New Testament is pervaded by an otherworldly apocalypticism that expected the world to end long before Rome fell. Moreover, slavery is accepted without condemnation, and slaves are urged to serve their masters in humble submission with gladness of heart. Process thinkers contend that God only persuades the world into greater harmony, while in the Bible God coerces nature and people from Genesis 1 to Revelation 21.

Let us look at those claims. To maintain that a critical feminist consciousness calling for full equality of the sexes in every aspect of secular and church life is a valid modernizing of the thought and practice of Jesus and of some early Christian communities is one thing. To maintain that this contemporary outlook defines the one and only true Gospel while at the same time insisting that the Bible is predominantly patriarchal is another thing. To urge that the emancipation of the oppressed from all forms of bondage is the supreme human task in response to divine love is a legitimate development of biblical themes is one thing. To claim that this is the essence of all genuine biblical religion is going too far. To claim that persuasive divine love is an appropriate contemporary rendering of the revelation of God in Jesus Christ is one thing. Even to suspect that the Whiteheadian God is identical with the Almighty Creator/King of Scripture is another.

Hence, would it not be better simply to say that we construct forms of religious life from the materials of the Christian past that are relevant for our time? Let us not claim that in so doing we have at last discovered or rediscovered its one and only vital core. The only way we can establish that against competing versions of the Gospel is to pound the desk and stomp the foot. Let us not say that our interpretation is the heart and center of biblical religion. Let us say it is the heart and center of our biblical religion. Scripture is our inspiration and guide. Let us not worry about some elusive essence that can only be defined by somebody in ways that will never claim universal assent.

Martin Luther found the heart of the Gospel to be salvation by grace through faith. James Cone finds it in the theme of God's liberating action on behalf of the oppressed. Elizabeth Schüssler Fiorenza finds it in the discipleship of equals in women's equalitarian church. Billy Graham finds it in the forgiveness of sins and the hope of heaven. All of that and more can be found in the Bible. Whether either of these it is the real heart of the objective Gospel is not resolvable. As interpreters, we become the functional authorities, no matter what we profess to be our objective norm. The relativist, pluralist, pragmatic modernist accepts that and lives with it. Jeffrey Stout says that being a pragmatist means never having to say you're certain. The modernist is at least relieved of that burden.

Homosexuality is being hotly debated today. Some liberal interpreters make a valiant effort to make it appear that, if properly understood, the Bible does not condemn responsible sexual relations between persons of the same sex, even in those very passages that seem to teach otherwise. One gets the impression that it is important to have textual biblical support for homosexual love or at least to render innocuous the offending verses. Exegetes who have, on some basis or another, come to believe that homosexuality is not wrong when practiced responsibly (using the same standards as apply to heterosexuals) work hard to find ways of softening or eliminating the biblical injunctions that appear to condemn homosexual activity. Maybe the words don't mean what they seem to mean. Maybe if we look at the text, the context, the translation of terms, and the like, we can take the offense out of the texts, while still accepting some validity to the injunction. This strategy may or may not be successful. Such exegesis may be correct. Why resort to it on theological or ethical grounds?

Do we know what various biblical writers or communities would have said about faithful, monogamous relationships among persons of the same sex? The more important point, however, is that any theological method that will allow particular moral issues like this to be settled by biblical exegesis alone is faulty. No question can be raised as to whether particular passages in the Bible advocate killing disobedient children (Deut. 21:18-21), or take slavery for granted, or forbid women to be teachers of men or to have authority over them (I Tim. 2:11-12). Do we regard these passages as authoritative for us? No, of course not. Then why should the morality of homosexual love be settled by reference to specific verses rather than by appeal to the highest ethical norms we know, having learned them from Scripture?

Only what in Scripture is irresistibly convincing to our own Christian reason in the light of what we cannot otherwise deny as modern human beings can be regarded as the authoritative Word of God for us. The modernist who takes this position can at least use the Bible with integrity and consistency. It will make it unnecessary to depend on texts that conform to what we already know or believe to be true, right, and good. Let us take responsibility for our convictions and not insist that we are merely reporting what the Bible teaches on the subject. The Bible is filled with various doctrines and perspectives. It is we who decide what among its many not always harmonious teachings is God's message for today.

Bernard Loomer once illustrated the point humorously. He was reading a scholarly paper at a conference. I don't recall what the point was he was emphasizing. Anyway, after reading a particular sentence, he stopped, looked out at the audience, and said, "As the Bible plainly teaches." He looked down, paused, looked out again, and said, "I don't know where, but it does." He looked back at his paper another time, waited a moment, looked up once more, and concluded, "Well, if it doesn't, it ought to!" Now there's a modernist after my own heart!

THE BIBLE AS KALEIDOSCOPE

Kaleidoscope comes from two Greek words meaning "beautiful form." The same pieces of glass produce a multitude of pretty patterns depending on how the instrument is turned. Does it make any sense to say that one of them is more right than the others? Doing theology is like playing with a kaleidoscope. We all read the same Bible and refer to the same classical texts from Tertullian to Barth. Many beautiful forms have been produced from Nicea to Trent and from Calvin and Luther to Tillich and Tracy, Cone and Cobb, Ruether and Suchocki. Which of these delightfully colored arrays of brilliant arrangements is the right one? The Bible is a kaleidoscope. Which beautiful form is seen depends on how it is turned. It is the same Bible, but we produce a bewildering variety of images, alike in many respects, different in many others. All have common colors. The arrangements are often only slightly at variance from others.

CONCLUSION

To conclude, we can claim to be Christians if what we believe is most conducive to human fulfillment is identical with what we take to be most excellent in the biblical witness. Moreover, the Bible is authoritative only because it is unsurpassed by anything else we know from any source. We are Christian because it is to the tradition of ancient Israel and the early church that we continue to look for a saving Word for the world of the late 20th century. We continue to look there because looking elsewhere has not yielded so rich a harvest of wisdom about life. We confess Jesus as the Christ because he is and has disclosed the Word that is nothing other than saving truth for us. We are Christians because it is to that tradition we turn, are compelled to turn, have no choice but to turn and return to, to argue with, to revise, to doubt and to reject, to transform and reinterpret, to be judged and transformed by. We read the Bible as Holy Scripture because of its unexcelled power to provide wisdom and a way of living that promises to make real the beauty and the goodness that life -- the gift of that Ultimate Mystery -- offers.

Chapter Five

Reconceiving God[1]

A concept of God can begin at many places. I begin with some questions about origins. What produced me? Where did the world come from? The reigning scientific theory informs us that the universe has evolved over billions of years from a "big bang."[1] But what is the *final* explanation of what went "bang"? Formally speaking, the answer to these questions is God, where God refers to what is actually ultimate. But who or what is God, and what is the relationship between God and the world? Is the world itself actually ultimate (God)? Did the presently actual world come from some past state of itself that has no beginning, or was it created by

---

[1] This chapter was presented in an earlier and shorter form as the Ayer Lecture at Colgate-Rochester/Bexley Hall/Crozer on April 3, 1991, under the title "Remythologizing God: An Experiment in Second Naïveté." It also forms part of Chapter V in my *Theological Biology* (Lewiston: The Edwin Mellen Press, 1991). Used by permission.

something more fundamental.² Maybe there was "nothing" before the present universe, and something just began to be.³ Perhaps some primordial chaos or energized potential generated from possibilities with itself initiated the present trajectory of becoming. Is Infinite Perfect Absolute Being or Undifferentiated Pure Nothingness the ultimate frame of reference in relation to which the world has its existence? Unless one believes that some relevant actuality is prior to every potentiality, everything can be thought away except possibility and "nothing," where "nothing" means the total absence of being, pure negation -- no being, no becoming. Possibility presumably just is.⁴ If so, what else is required to produce the world we live in? Speculative thought at this level provides no certainty. Agnosticism is the only defensible posture for human beings with regard to Ultimate Mystery. Nevertheless, it is useful for purposes of understanding and for coping with life to have some workable theory about ultimates based on our experience of what the actual world is like and might reasonably require as its final explanation.⁵

What is it that a doctrine of God needs to account for? What clues are provided in our experience of the world that are suggestive of the nature and character of the Ultimate Fact? The answer is two-fold.

1. **The Emergence and Evolution of Life:** The evolutionary process has produced multitudinous forms of life. Organisms are highly organized systems composed of mutually sustaining, interacting parts whose harmonious functioning sustains the life of the whole in ways that tend to actualize the potential within it. The processes of life are internally directed toward the survival and flourishing of the individual organism and the perpetuation of the species. The universe appears to have a life-producing, life-fulfilling, and life-reproducing urge and capacity. Moreover, new forms of life have emerged over long periods of time hinting at a tendency toward novel complexity aimed at increasing the range and depth of possible experiences.⁶ The process that produced the first living cell and finally eventuated in the appearance of human beings with their marvelous capacities for thinking, feeling, and

creating indicates a purposive element at work in the cosmos that requires explanation.

However, the peculiar nature of the evolutionary process also poses questions that a doctrine of God must answer. Species have emerged in what appears to be a blind, groping manner not in a fashion that points to an intelligent purpose with a definite plan. Moreover, the dysteleological aspects are appalling, calling into question the goodness of God. Many observers have noted the happenstance, contingency, waste, cruelty, death, and horror of the proceedings and the apparent indifference of the process to the weak and helpless, allowing the strong to survive and the unadapted to perish.

2. The Goodness of Existence: Life is experienced as potentially and essentially good, i. e. capable of producing enjoyable, desirable, and satisfying experiences. The processes of life that fulfill the potential of the organism are experienced as pleasing and agreeable. It is good to be. Goodness is coincident with being.[7] Life with its promise of happiness and joy is a gift to us from some Ultimate Mystery. The delight and ecstasy of life at its best point toward a Loving Giver of what comes to us a pure unmerited favor, grace.

Hence, the emergence of life, its evolution toward novel forms of complexity, and its goodness require explication by reference to primordial factors prior to and resident in the cosmic process. A theory is needed that explains the experienced world and our own experience of what it is to be a living, thinking, feeling being. My intuition is that the universe is in the business of producing life and promoting its fulfillment. Life is the process of the possible becoming actual under the lure and drive of the good. Hence, I project this observation and experience into the primordial situation as a way of developing a doctrine of God explanatory of the experienced world.

I conclude that the cosmos exhibits patterns of meaning and purpose that suggest that at the base of all things is a Creativity that has the character of goodness, best described as love. As a Christian, I believe this to be the heart of the biblical witness. As a philosopher, I believe that the fact of evolving life and its experienced quality of goodness can plausibly be explained by reference to a trinity of factors incorporated into a di-polar version of naturalistic panentheism. At the same time, the nature of the evolutionary process points to an opportunistic Creativity with loving intentions but with limited power and capability and not to an omnipotent, omnicompetent Perfection.

A DI-POLAR GOD

In the evolution of the cosmos over billions of years, something new has been produced. This suggests a distinction between the Created (our actual evolving world) and the Uncreated (the primordial condition explanatory of its emergence).[8] Perhaps the Uncreated is "absolutely nothing," and by some absolute, inexplicable contingency, something began to be. Maybe the Uncreated is pure possibility. Yet mere possibility seems insufficient to account for the emergence of something real. The view I find most satisfactory is that the Uncreated Factors are Eros, Possibility, and The Good.[9] Eros (Desire) is the powerful, active urge to actualize Possibility in quest of The Good. Possibility refers to whatever can be or become.[10] The Good is Ideal Possibility or what normatively fulfills or satisfies Eros.[11] Eros unites with Possibility in quest of The Good to generate the most primitive sequence of actualities that could arise *ex nihilo* from pure potentiality.[12] In some sequence the possible begins to become actual under the lure of The Good and the drive of Eros. Hence, there emerges the space-time/matter continuum and with it the evolving cosmic process that has brought the presently actual world into being. Somewhere in this process occurs the "big bang" that scientists describe as the beginning of our cosmic era. This emergent process (the world) is what I call the Created. Metaphorically, the world is the Body of God.

God, then, is the name given to the di-polar reality that includes the Uncreated and the Created. The Uncreated is the Primordial Ground or Cause of the Created. The Created is the novelty that emerges in time and in the processive cosmos. It is the universe produced and being produced by the Uncreated Factors to which we have no epistemic access, except through what is experienciable. The Created is both God and is in God. I propose, then, to add to the conversation a form of naturalistic panentheism. The world is in God, but is not, as such, the whole of God. To identify God with the World as a Whole, as Bernard Loomer does, is to unify the Uncreated and the Created into one concrete reality.[13]

In this form of empirical theism, God created the world and us. This means that factors ontologically and temporally prior to the presently actual world account for our existence and for the possibility of meaningful life. God is our Cosmic Parent, our Heavenly Mother-Father. Following the earlier empirical theists, an organism-environment scheme will be employed as a useful way of organizing our experience and giving us a comprehensive frame of reference. We are organisms living in an immediate environment of time and space and nature that sustains our bodies. God is the name for the Cosmic Environment in which "we live and move and have our being" (Acts 17:28 RSV). As far as he went, Shailer Mathews was on a useful track with his definition of God as the concept we have of "the personality-producing, personality-sustaining factors in the cosmos."[14]

Let us, then, assume a distinction between the Uncreated and the Created. Uniting these aspects, but keeping them in mind, let us proceed. God is a Cosmic Organism in whom Eros has woven on the frame of space-time/matter-energy a world, actualizing its potential in quest of Possible Good or Ideal Possibility. The Evolving World is the Created. The Uncreated factors are Eros, Possibility and The Good or Eros and Ideal Possibility. The space-time/matter-energy continuum is a product of their union, and it may have an infinite past. Mythically, I imagine that Space-Time is the first (logical if not chronological) child of Eros-impregnated Ideal Possibility. Symbolically, God may be considered as a Cosmic Life whose aim at self-realization is also an aim at self-realization for all sub-societies and individuals within the Divine Body. God is both the All-Embracing Society and the Universal Individual.[15]

GOD AS PERSON

We have no way to determine whether God is everlastingly conscious, an emergent consciousness, conscious only in finite consciousness, or not conscious at all. God can be imagined metaphorically as a Cosmic Person whose body is the world. In other contexts, God can be thought of as the Mind of the cosmos. While we have no compelling basis for saying that such a Mind or Person exists as a self-conscious subject of experience, we do have experiential reasons to affirm that God is present to and operative in experience as if God were a self-conscious experiencing Person. Life is experienced as a good gift from God. Possibilities of meaning and enjoyment are generated in life processes that are cosmically produced. Pragmatically, it would be the same in terms of the events of real life in all its public and private dimensions if God were an intelligent, purposive, conscious, feeling Person.

The world process can be described, then, as the possible becoming actual under the lure of the good. Eros is the hunger for actualizing potential that yields satisfaction or enjoyment. It is the driving energy that pushes the process into creative advance.[16] The Cosmic Organism is driven by Eros in quest of the Good to actualize what is possible. Or God may be described as the Life of the World, where life means the process by which potential is actualized in accordance with internally guided ends. This Adventurous Life is in the process of realizing the potential of the cosmos. Internally driven by Eros in quest of The Good, the Body of God lives and grows. Organisms, whether God or goldfish, are driven by eros "to live, to live well, and to live better."[17] God may be metaphorically described as the World as a Whole struggling to actualize to the fullest in variety and qualitative richness the potential of the Primeval Atom as it exploded and evolved into the expanding galaxies and into earth's biological evolutionary spectacle. God is the Cosmic Life in whom we live our lives.[18]

In short, the doctrine of God sketched above in an imaginative construct that seeks to account for the presently actual world by reference to the underlying factors that constitute the realm of ultimacy. I cannot think away Possibility (the sum total of all entities and arrangements individually and in all combinations that could become actual). However, mere Possibility cannot generate a creative process of becoming. That role is played by Eros, the hunger (desire) for actualization that fulfills. Whatever fulfills desire is good. For there to be a continuing process of creation in which actualities are organized harmoniously in ways that enable emergent actualities to survive and prosper, reference must be made to The Good. The Good is the principle of ideal organization and progressive actualization. Primordially, with "nothing" to build on, I imagine that the first or an early emergent was space-time sequentially evolving into the space-time/matter-energy continuum the emerging cosmic process that produced on earth human beings who could wonder where they came from. At each stage in very moment and situation, the presently actual sets the limits of what is possible, i e., what can become actual, in the immediate future.

SPEAKING OF GOD

Symbol, image, and metaphor are being used with no particular discrimination among them. Analogy might have been used as well. The precise definition of each in relation to the other is a matter of considerable controversy. Is symbol different from metaphor and analogy or identical with the one in contrast to the other or a general term encompassing both plus perhaps other non-literal attributions?[19] Disputes about the matter cannot be resolved. We do not know, cannot know, the exact way in which our language does or not correspond to or correctly describe in some fashion the objective referent. Metaphors, symbols, and images specify an element in our interpreted experience of God. They point to God as experienced and believed in. They relate something felt as God to the whole of our experienced and interpreted world. They are valid for us if they function effectively in that way. Precise definitions and discriminations among the variety of non-literal references to God may be useful for some purpose.[20] It will be sufficient for the present purpose to say that these terms indicate similarity between some known finite reality and the experienced reality of God. More precisely, they suggest a likeness or identity in one or more respects between the symbol and that which is symbolized but unlikeness in other respects.

A myth presents a set of religious and philosophical convictions in the form of a story about the gods. To talk of God as a Person who thinks, feels, and acts like a human being and who does things in the world is to use language mythically. Ordinary language, including anthropological terms, referring to finite realities are employed to interpret experienced aspects about God or ultimate facts. Myths are not literally true, of course, but they articulate felt meanings that function pragmatically as if they were. They intend to point to something really present in the objective sphere that cannot be precisely expressed in the vocabulary used. Mythological statements do not misrepresent the ultimate situation in so far as the significance of reality for our experience is concerned. They are existentially adequate and religiously useful though not conceptually exact. My myths assume the world-picture of present-day science as incorporated into a philosophical scheme that intends to explicate the religious meaning of reality as experienced.

We cannot be sure how accurately our myths, concepts, and metaphors describe objective reality. We can live by the faith that reality as experienced is not misrepresented by our functionally operative theories. Our language is not misleading and, therefore, not untrue in the pragmatic sense. If it functions to provide understanding and a way of coping with life that leads to the actualization of the potential for meaning and enjoyment, it is validated. The most adequate religious vision would be that one that led to the maximal actualization of the possibilities for justice and happiness in this world. It may be that a plurality of visions may function equally well in this regard. In so, they are equally true if they meet all the standards of theoretical and practical reason within the perspectives that sponsor them and for the persons who believe them and live by them. This does not mean that anything goes or that every belief is a good as any other. We must stand by and even fight for, at whatever level of defense or offense is appropriate, those values produced by religious visions that are essential in our minds to justice and human happiness.

Does this view lead to an indefensible relativism? Does it make any practical difference whether we believe our way of looking at things corresponds with objective reality and that contrary views are wrong or whether we are just sufficiently subjectively convinced of our views when it comes to working wholeheartedly for their realization and appropriately resisting what is believed to be evil and destructive of justice and well-being? It appears to me that it is the strength of conviction itself based on compelling reasons that is finally determinative, not whether objectivist or relativist views of truth are held. Theologians and philosophers may aim at objective truth and intend their views to correspond with reality. The problem is that we cannot be sure when belief and knowledge coincide. But when issues of justice and injustice arise, we have to fight for the good and the right as we see it *as if* we were in possession of the truth.

While we cannot prove our propositions, we can give an accounting of how we and/or our culture came to have these convictions and offer evidence to show that living by them is preferable compared to the alternatives. I know of no way to escape relativism with respect to the ultimate questions of God and the good, where relativism means that the only means of justification are those available to us in our own culture or freshly invented by ourselves. Granted many would willingly instruct me in the way beyond the dilemma of objectivism and relativism, but I have yet to be convinced that any proposed resolution does the job. Usually, the opponents of relativism win by declaring that they have. Besides the great thinkers propose different ways, so I still have to make a subjective choice among them, since I do not know how to determine which one is objectively true. The deeper question, perhaps, is whether relativism when embraced does not inevitably lead to a loss of passionate commitment. How can one give oneself without reserve to something unless one is pretty sure that the supporting belief is really true? I believe that it is enough for people to be convinced of the meaningfulness of life and that the ideas and values they hold are important enough to live by, to promote, and to defend. Maybe it differs from person to person. Anyway, since any kind of final certainty is not possible for me, only some kind of relativism is an option, regardless.

A GOD WHO ACTS

We can speak mythically of God as an Agent working in the world, striving and suffering with it, creating, judging, and redeeming its creatures, and directing all things toward fulfillment. Translated into concepts, this means that in and through the structures and processes of nature and history as a whole and its parts, a creative purpose is present. When we assert that God acts purposefully in the world, we point to a *telos* that is present in things. Eros is active by which the possible becomes actual under the lure of the good. When we speak of God acting, we refer to the goal-seeking activities in nature, the inner-directedness in things that drives them toward an end.[21] Nature discloses a capacity for creating new organic wholes capable of more complex forms of functioning. Emergent evolution is the story of the creativity and purposiveness that unfolds in cosmic and earthly history. Component parts serve as means by which the aims of an organism to live and to strive for fulfillment are achieved. The molecules, cells, organs, and systems of organs within living beings function cooperatively and interdependently to achieve the goals of the organism as a whole while mutually sustaining each other.

Purposes pervade the workings of nature. When we say that God acts, we refer to this *telic* dimension in the world. God works in and through the whole system of nature with the aim of actualizing the potential for enjoyment in organisms large and small. God's aim for all finite creatures is to increase the quality, intensity, and richness of experience. God's will seeks pleasure, enjoyment, justice, happiness for all human beings. God wants to increase loving relationships within the community of persons and between all people and Her/Himself. All processes that increase richness of experience and enjoyment are the work of God. This includes what went on in the first few seconds after the "big bang" by which the course of cosmic evolution was set. It embraces what occurred when hydrogen was turned into helium. Later God was at work in the hot, deep interior of stars producing the heavier elements essential to life on earth.[22] In short, the primordial union of Eros, Possibility, and The Good generates a creative process that functions at the border of structure and surprise, order and chaos, stable pattern and adventurous novelty to unfold the spectacle of cosmic evolution and the historical emergence of life and humankind.

Put simply, to say that God acts means that we detect purposiveness in the world that is accounted for by reference to a Final Fact. God has *a general purpose* to actualize possibility in quest of the good and *particular purposes* for particular occasions to increase enjoyment in living beings. God is involved as Ultimate Ground wherever an occurrence takes place that contributes to the achieving of those purposes. In short, the story of life and its evolution can be told mythically in terms of the outworking of Cosmic Personal Purpose.

Speaking mythically, God's *special* work is generating the cooperative response in creatures that is necessary to actualize the potential for enjoyment given with the gift of life. God's *general* work is creating the foundational structures and processes that make life and its fulfillment possible. Both the *special* and the *general* work are mediated through the eros in all life that drives it toward the good. At the human level, conscious discernment of divine purpose can facilitate a cooperative response that enables people to attune themselves to the divine intention. They can strive opportunistically with the facts of life to maximize creative possibilities despite the threat of destructive evils and frustrating ambiguities. Christians respond to God by preaching the Gospel and demonstrating love that seeks justice.

GOD AND EVIL

Life is an adventure full of promise but also full of peril. Good and evil are both part of our experience. Evil is the frustration or destruction of a potential for enjoyment in living beings. It is experienced as suffering. Two types of evil need to be distinguished, depending on whether it does or does not involve human irresponsibility.[23]

1. **NATURAL EVIL:** We are complex organisms dependent on the healthy functioning of all systems and subsystems that make up the body. Something can go wrong. We are vulnerable to accident, disease, and all kinds of malfunctioning. This suffering arises from the nature of things and involves no human irresponsibility. Natural evil in a possibility inherent in *finitude*.

2. **MORAL EVIL:** Because we are self-determining beings, we can do harm to each other by bad intent or through carelessness. This involves human irresponsibility. Moral evil is a possibility inherent in *freedom*.

Evil arises when sentient organisms (1) fail to achieve or lose organized stability and/or maximum actualization of their potential for enjoyment for internal reasons or (2) undergo destructive conflicts with entities external to them. Evil, then, in the comprehensive sense is the disruption or destruction of a potential for enjoyment in sentient beings. Hence, evil is not primordial but emergent and occurs when a possibility for good is frustrated or destroyed. Given the nature of finitude and the complexity of organization that enjoyment in organisms requires, evil can and will most probably occur. Sentient beings are vulnerable to destruction because of internal failure and external conflict.

Theodicy deals with the problem of evil in relation to God. Usually it is an attempt to show that it is possible to affirm the omnipotence of God, the love of God, and the reality of evil without contradiction. The skeptic's argument generally is that given the reality of evil, we must sacrifice either the power (omnipotence) or the love (goodness) of God. A dilemma arises. If we give up the omnipotence of God, it appears that God cannot prevent or overcome evil. If we forego the goodness it seems that God will not prevent or overcome evil. Most theodicies attempt to show that this dilemma is only apparent and that it is possible to affirm both God is all-powerful and perfectly loving, despite the presence of real evil in the world.

Before we proceed, we must note that some Christian theologians refuse to accept the definition of the problem in these terms. They argue that evil is a practical reality that requires resources that enable us to deal with it and overcome it. This the Gospel provides to those who have faith and seek to love God and one another. These theologians contend that to define evil as a theoretical question that poses difficulties regarding either the existence or the character of God is to take a false step and one that leads to no good consequences. Hence, this solution of the theodicy question is to deny that it is a theoretical problem in the first instance and therefore does not require a solution in these terms. Another way to put it is to say that they are quite willing to let the question of reconciling the reality of evil with the power and goodness of God remain as pure MYSTERY and devote their full attention to the question of coping with evil in good faith.

Other theologians agree that evil is indeed a practical concern. Of course, they argue, we need resources that enable us to cope with it. However, they contend that suffering also has a theoretical dimension. Faith must seek understanding as well as victory over evil. These thinkers typically proceed to offer a number of "appeals" that lessen if not eliminate the contradiction. Some of the "appeals" most often made are:

1. Suffering is a punishment for sin.
2. We are creatures of flesh and blood who are vulnerable to accident, disease, and other destructive assaults upon our well-being.
3. We are free moral beings who misuse our freedom to cause harm to ourselves and others.
4. Suffering is designed by God be a part of the world so that by facing the challenge evil poses, we can freely move toward moral perfection, which is God's purpose for us.
5. We live in a world containing a plurality of interacting beings. Hence, it is inevitable that destructive consequences will occur. But it is only because nature has a law-abiding character that we can learn and carry out our purposes.
6. Satan (a superhuman being with free will who went wrong) is the cause of much evil and suffering in the world.

From such "appeals" one can argue that given these factors, evil and suffering will likely follow. Yet some of them are essential to there being a world at all or are required by the excellence of its design. For example, the fact that God made us free is a good feature of the world that we would not want to change. But it means that human beings and Satan who misuse that freedom cause great misery. In short, any good world would carry with it the possibility of evil. Therefore, if there is to be a world at all and a good world, evil is a highly probable feature of it, but this does not at all impugn either the power or the goodness of God.

Those who make them believe that these "appeals" go a long way toward providing an answer to the question as to why there is so much evil in the world that an all-powerful, loving God created. Most admit, however, that we are still far from a complete solution. Hence, the final "appeal" is usually to MYSTERY. At this point, they join with those who refuse to see evil as a theoretical issue in the first place.

Not every theologian uses all these "appeals." Many modern thinkers, e. g., would not refer to suffering as a punishment for sin, and many do not believe in a literal Satan.

In my mind these traditional responses are inadequate. My view is that we must limit the power God in order to preserve the goodness of God. This means that I reluctantly accept the consequences of compromising the omnipotence of God. I believe that the reason that God does not prevent or overcome some suffering is that God cannot. Only a Suffering, Struggling, Limited God will do.

To elaborate, the evil we know in this life consists of real suffering and injustice along with the evil constituted by the good that might have been but is not. Evils abundant are interwoven with good in a fabric of complex ambiguity and rooted in a combination of the sinful, the demonic, and the tragic.[24] If we abandon classical theism, what hypothesis about God is theoretically required, or at least pragmatically permitted, by an interpretation based on our experience of the world we live in here and now? Theory can be satisfied with a number of alternatives. One can account for much evil by qualifying the divine power, or goodness, or wisdom. To put it in simple, ordinary language, God might be:

1. perfectly good and unlimited in power but dumb, **or**
2. perfectly good and supremely intelligent but weak, **or**
3. infinitely wise and almighty but with a mean streak, **or**
4. lacking in two or all of these perfections.

Speculative reason is suspended among these alternatives with no compelling reason to prefer one to the others.[25] There are, however, experiential and pragmatic reasons for believing that God is perfect in intention but lacking in the ability to actualize either (a) the most excellent world possible in principle or (b) a perfect world free of all evil in fact. This hypothesis cannot, of course, be proven. One cannot even demonstrate its theoretical superiority over other options. It is finally a matter of intuition, of a hunch about what is going on. We live by faith. We "see through a glass darkly." My intuition about ultimate things rests on the experience that it is good to be, that life is a gift that is potentially and essentially excellent, worthwhile, desirable, and marvelously wonderful. I conclude that the Cosmic Giver of Life is unbounded love whose intention is to create a world and to actualize as much of its potential for meaningful enjoyment as possible. This goal is worked out within a context of ultimate and immediate conditions that constrain what can be done. Hence, I believe God is perfectly loving but limited in power.

None of the traditional theodicies is satisfying. It is not that they lack merit. Especially the appeal to the nature of finitude and the reality of freedom go a long way toward absolving Omnipotent Love from guilty or direct responsibility for evil. Nevertheless, after all the insight they contain is added up, they leave too much unexplained on the basis of their initial assumptions. They end up one way or the other rationalizing the bad away in deference to divine perfection or acknowledging defeat by resort to mystery and divine transcendence when experience contradicts their attempted resolution. Sometimes they put the blame back on us. We lack faith or virtue. We have the wrong attitudes toward life and so on. The realities of life and the testimony of experience justify attempts to formulate alternatives to the traditional theodicies. This world is not equal in excellence in principle and in structure to some possible world. A completely perfect finite world (one with abundant good and no evil) does not seem to be possible. Nor does this world seem to be a path toward some eventual perfection. The hope that God will in the end miraculously rid the world of natural and moral ills, seems improbable. These are intuitions and hunches, not assured knowledge or demonstrable theses. This world, of course, could be factually better than it is, had a different set of contingent events occurred and a different set of free decisions been made. Nevertheless, a world better in basic design seems possible, one that would be more likely to produce a greater net gain of good over evil, even if it would not be free of all afflictions whatsoever.[26]

Only a suffering God will do. More precisely, only a finite, struggling, suffering, loving God will suffice pragmatically to account for the experienced good of this life in the midst of ambiguity and evil. The affirmation that at the base of things lies a perfect intention of love to create life and to direct it toward fulfillment provides a framework for human commitment, for religious devotion, and for moral action. Our worship and work consist in responding in gratitude and praise to the divine intention by aligning our own efforts with the striving of God to create a community of loving persons who live happily in a just, harmonious, and prosperous society.[27]

The idea of God as Creative Suffering, Struggling Love affords a basis for faith and ethics, i. e., a life of worship and a life of active good works. Moreover, the idea of a finite God perfect in intention but not in power fits well with the known facts about cosmic and biological evolution. The spectacle that before our wondering eyes does appear gives evidence of purpose. The universe appears to be in the business of creating life in as many varieties as the environment will permit. Moreover, time displays a one-way trajectory that has an upward thrusting push toward organisms of greater complexity. These more highly developed life-forms are capable or wider ranges and depths of experience and of potential enjoyment than their simpler ancestors and contemporaries.

The cosmic process has produced human beings with the strange habit and ability to ask from whence all this comes and what it all means. These beings have a capacity for a qualitative richness and density of complex experience unique to the creatures of earth. They can love each other, create and enjoy great music, invent religious visions of the origin and destiny of all things, set forth high standards of conduct for themselves and others, and do all sorts of other wonderful things. Yet the height of their creativity in increasing the joy of life is matched by their destructive tendencies by which violence and hate cover the earth to their shame. The cosmos must have in it "personality-producing capacities" (Mathews), since it has in fact produced persons.[28] Yet the evolutionary process seems more opportunistic in producing what it can under the circumstances, rather than having the ability to produce some definite outcome. I do not believe we can account for the blind, clumsy, groping character of evolution and the apparent waste, contingency, cruelty, conflict, and pain exhibited in the process except by a doctrine of a finite God. People were invented by the process. We have no assurance that this was the predetermined consequence of some omnipotent aim. Purpose is immanent *in* the cosmos. The evidence does not sustain belief in a purpose *for* the process, i. e., some foreordained end that will in good time come to pass no matter what. More specifically, the cosmos, or at least planet earth, seems to be the story of the emergence of life in abundance, life with varying capacities for experiencing the goodness inherent in being. If life has not appeared beyond the earth, it is because the requisite conditions have not been present. Nevertheless, a persistent and deep Eros in the very matrix of becoming hungers to lure the possible into reality with the intent of maximizing richness of experience felt as enjoyment. The forms that life takes, or whether it develops at all, depends on circumstances. The Creative Purpose at work in the cosmos is real but limited in its capacities to bring to happy fulfillment the creatures it thrusts from its fecund womb. Hence, the process is ambiguous, a mixture of good and evil, of pain and pleasure, of success and failure, of creation and destruction, and -- in Christian imagery -- of crucifixion and resurrection.

GOD AND HOPE

Finally, the concept of a loving but limited and opportunistic God provides a realistic basis for hope that can be tested by experience. An empirical theology of history will be based on three assumptions:

(1) The structures and processes operative in nature and history now are the same as those that have been present throughout the human past.

(2) The principles to be employed in understanding the past are to be derived from an interpretation of experience in the present.[29]

(3) Human experience here and now when critically interpreted reveal no exceptions to the general structures, processes, and possibilities present in everyday events in the world.[30]

A contemporary empirical theology of history will include the following points.

1. The cosmic process has created human beings with a moral consciousness and a hunger for a better life. Thus endowed, humanity over the centuries has produced visions of justice and of the good and of the better set forth as norms and goals of human behavior. For Christians the imperative of counting the neighbor's need and good equal to one's own can hardly be improved on. Also unsurpassable is the definition of the goal of life as a community united by praise of God and love of neighbor -- the Commonwealth of God. This norm and this goal reflect aims ingredient in the creativity at the base of things. The fact of human moral and teleological consciousness in its highest reaches provides evidence of a purposive God whose character is love.

2. A plausible interpretation of thousands of years of human experience yields the conclusion that moral progress is potential in the historical process while not certain or inevitable. The past and the present are ambiguous, a mixture of good and evil. The future is unpredictable and likely to be remain ambiguous for reasons offered by Reinhold Niebuhr and Bernard Loomer.[31] History exhibits patterns of moral advance and of moral regression, as well as of stagnation and inertia. Yet in the midst of this some patterns of genuine progress are undeniable.[32] Contrary to some current liberation and eschatological theologies, it is unrealistic to suppose that social perfection will be reached on earth somehow, sometime by a mighty deed of God or by a combination of divine and human action.[33] Likewise, the liberal hope for a gradual movement of society toward peace, justice, harmony, and well-being is too simplistic.

The dialectic of Reinhold Niebuhr is more convincing. On the one hand, history exhibits indeterminate possibilities for good; no prior limits can be put on the extent to which justice may be achieved in society and to which love may become the ruling norm of individual lives. On the other hand, any achieved good can be corrupted and lost; fresh outbreaks of evil are possible. Moreover, the perils rise with the promises so that greater possibilities of good bring greater possibilities of evil. Since sin springs from freedom at the depths of the human spirit, it is an ever present possibility. Hence, no accumulation of social gains can ever guarantee the full and final triumph of righteousness. Yet every situation contains some potential for greater justice, harmony, and human fulfillment that we are obliged to achieve.

3. In particular, *kairotic* moments appear in history produced by a convergence of factors that create a potential "*Gestalt* of grace" whose actualization can at least partially overcome the reign of the demonic (Tillich).[34] In language more congenial to process-relational thought, now and then right and ripe moments appear full of new possibilities of justice, peace, prosperity, and joyful self-realization. These are occasions of hopeful opportunity calling for midwives of the divine Commonwealth to facilitate the birth of the new and better reality with which history is pregnant.

While prior human activity is the proximate creator of these novel potentials of fulfillment, the ultimate source lies in the objective nature of things. The ground of hope is the creativity of God by which goodness itself is real and new possibilities of its actualization emerge when certain conditions are present. Human beings did not originally create themselves. Neither did they create the capacity for enjoyment resident in all living beings. In the greater cosmic scheme, then, human action, strictly speaking, can only actualize possibilities of good latent in the givenness of things. That justice as possibility exists is a God-given fact and not a human creation, although its embodiment in particular situations is.

A pregnant moment of history occurred in the 18th century that gave birth to democratic government and ideals of human rights to life, liberty, equality, and the pursuit of happiness. Another transpired in the mid-twentieth century that gave rise to the Civil Rights Movement led by Martin Luther King, Jr. Doubtless other potential leaders as ably equipped and as committed as King had come along earlier, but the time was not ripe. In previous eras they would have been crushed immediately by the reigning demonic powers.

4. Hope is expectation that some appropriate good will be actualized in a situation in which the chances lie somewhere between impossibility and certainty. As a subjective attitude, it may be strong or weak, either because of or in spite of the objective probabilities. A distinction can be made between two overlapping and interdependent forms of hope. *Realistic hope* is contextual, particular, and more concrete. It relates to a real potential in a given situation in the near term. *Utopian hope* is non-contextual, general, and more abstract. It pertains to what is logically possible without regard to whether the means for actualizing it are presently understood or available. It is a wish that no one yet knows how to make come true but which could come true if the right steps were taken. The hope that the human race can live in perpetual peace in circumstances of ideal justice under sustainable conditions of prosperity in which no one lacks the material goods and social opportunities to live a long, healthy, and happy life is utopian. The hope that a national health insurance plan can be achieved in the United States in the next few years that will provide basic and catastrophic medical care to all is realistic.

Realistic hope is for the short run. Goals and strategies can be specified in some detail with reasonable expectation of success but with no guarantee. It defines the immediate tasks. *Utopian hope* is for the long run -- the stuff of dreams. It defines the ultimately desirable that is eventually possible but for which no set of steps can be laid out that would achieve the goal. In its widest and highest reaches *utopian hope* yearns for the absolute ideal. It imagines at its acme the nearest thing to perfection that is possible, even wishing for the perfect itself, even if it is not fully possible in terms we can understand. *Realistic hope* needs to be nourished, sustained, and guided by *utopian hope* lest it become too timid, weak, and complacent. *Utopian hope* needs to be held in check and balanced by *realistic hope* lest it degenerate into mere daydreaming that neglects the real potentials at hand. *Utopian hope* too long unrealized can begin to look like an illusion and may turn into despair. These two forms of hope form an unbroken continuum and flow into each other, so that a clear demarcation is impossible.[35] The form and content of each vary with time, place, and circumstance. Isaiah 11:1-9 and Revelation 21:1-4, as well as I Corinthians 15: 24-28, 51-55, are instances of *utopian hope* from earlier eras. Each arises out of a particular situation but reach out to embrace an absolute future void of evil.

5. In empirical theism hope cannot rest on the proposition that history will be perfected on earth at some indefinite future by a mighty coercive act of God. In fact, the hope of eventual perfection here or hereafter cannot be a matter of basic doctrine, although such a belief may be entertained as an uncertain possibility. In the present theology the notion of *utopian hope* occupies the place that the expectation of a perfect social order inaugurated by an act of divine will. This form of hope held in more orthodox views, including many contemporary eschatological and liberation theologies, has been invalidated by historical fact. None of the expected promises of a perfected social order whether in the Old Testament or the New have been fulfilled. The actual history recorded by the Bible itself is evidence enough, not to mention the nearly two thousand years that have ensued since. The scoffers who challenged the author of II Peter in the second century were right then, and they are still right: "For ever since the fathers fell asleep, all things have continued as they were from the beginning of creation" (3:4 RSV).

To hold that the events referred to in biblical eschatologies are yet to come it is to stretch exegesis beyond reasonable bounds. To suggest that an alternate version it is literally true except for the time frame it is a desperate expedient that misses the point of the mythology in which they are contained. The biblical myths must be taken as a whole and reinterpreted as a whole, not broken into pieces so that what has not been refuted can be preserved intact while discarding the rest.

The Bible assumes that a perfect or at least a very good world existed in the beginning (Gen. 1-3) and that a new, transformed, and unambiguously good world will be established at the end (Roms. 8:18-28; I Cor. 15; Rev. 21: 1-4). Modern eschatologies readily give up the notion of a paradise in the past. Science and historical evidence have refuted the notion. Yet liberal, neo-orthodox, and liberation theologies alike hold in various ways to the hope that the world and a righteous remnant of persons will be perfected at a divinely-wrought consummation. In contrast, a modern *Gestalt* it is offered here that reinterprets the biblical *Gestalt*. Perfection at the beginning it is replaced by ambiguous potential, while hope it is held out for a better but not a perfected future. Disaster for the human race on earth cannot be ruled out. Neither can a future here or in a heaven beyond that embodies a good so wondrous that human imagination cannot now discern its form and details. The ultimate possibilities for the future disappear into mysteries beyond human comprehension. Hope outruns the facts presently available to us and carries no guarantees for anything beyond the moment.

More concretely and specifically, in any given situation in which we find ourselves, history it is pregnant with possibilities for good. Our task it is to discern and actualize them and, when we cannot, to play our hunches and commit our lives to the most promising and probable prospects. In faith and hope beyond the facts, we live our lives, yet respecting the facts when they are known. In some immediate circumstances, there it is no hope for what we want most or even for what would be best, all things considered. People get sick, and sick people die. Oppression and violence crush lives right and left. Yet when the context it is sufficiently widened or narrowed,[36] hopeful possibilities emerge even from the worst of presents, allowing us to make the most of them when and if we can. Reality is relentless, inexorable, and ruthless. Often the best possible in a given situation it is not very good. The lives of the tender-hearted must always be tinged with sadness and a sense of the tragic. Yet life can be very good and can nearly always be made better. No more and no less it is the meaning of hope.

CONCLUSION

Do I have any reason to believe that these ideas are true? My answer it is that I do not find the notion of as correspondence to reality useful when dealing with ultimate matters. How could one possibly test theories about God to assign marks of true or false to them and get any results that one could be certain about? Rival doctrines confront and eliminate each other in endless rounds of debate. I am a pragmatist. Theories are worthy of belief by particular persons if they are useful to them in accounting for known relevant evidence in the most compelling fashion and in providing a way of coping with life's problems and challenges. Theories can be tested in life in terms whether in the light of all considerations they sustain themselves as coherent doctrines that harmoniously integrate available evidence in the most productive way and lead to satisfying consequences. Theories become more plausible if they fit with all our other beliefs and lead to further insights that can be incorporated into a consistent whole. Obviously, some interpreter collects the evidence, puts it together in a theory, and tests it by stated criteria. We cannot judge whether such theories correspond to reality, but we can make tentative claims about their usefulness in promoting understanding and the good life for all. The only thing one can claim it is that a theory about God represents the best one knows from all available sources up to now, while remaining open to further insight. Exponents of competing doctrines can engage in conversation, critically and constructively conducted, in search of mutual edification that leads all parties toward greater appreciation of each and toward more profound theoretical constructions. The conception of God so fragmentarily developed on these pages sustains itself in my thinking to the extent that it can usefully organize the totality of my experience in coherent fashion and provide a way of coping with life in a satisfactory way.

Notes

1. See Stephen Hawking, *A Brief History of Time* (New York: Bantam Books, 1988).
2. Ibid., 115-41. Hawking's interpretation of present scientific evidence is that the universe is self-existent and has no beginning nor end. Shifting into philosophical mode, he then wonders what need we have of a Creator. However, a theologian may be forgiven for noting that the great physicist seems to be innocent of all views of God except a deistic one. For more speculation about the implications of the "big bang" for the existence of God, see William Lane Craig and Quinton Smith, *Theism, Atheism, and Big Bang Cosmology* (New York: Oxford University Press, 1993).
3. See the discussion by Paul Tillich, *Systematic Theology* (Chicago: University of Chicago Press, 1951), I:186-9. Here I intend the absolute nothingness presupposed in the Christian doctrine of *creatio ex nihilo*, the guarantee in orthodoxy of the complete sovereignty of God. Since there was "nothing" over against God, no power or being in addition to God that could resist the divine will.
4. The distinction between abstract logical possibility, i. e., anything conceivable, meaning anything not self-contradictory, on the one hand, and real potentiality, i. e., something for which the essential conditions for actualizing some possibility are present here and now, on the other hand, may be relevant here. Perhaps we need only be concerned practically about real potentials. Yet must not even possibility as abstract logical possibility have some ontological status? Possibility is more than pure nothingness and less than real being. Is not its status eternal and necessary? It is difficult to imagine possibility becoming possible. Wasn't the possible always possible (eternally in a non-temporal sense) and necessary?
5. For a more detailed examination of possibilities, see my *Theological Biology* (Lewiston: Edwin Mellen Press, 1991), 234-7.
6. I am persuaded that all fundamental entities (individuals and organic societies) that compose the universe are life-like and that life and experience are universal categories that apply at every level of existence in some sense. Referring in the most literal and proper sense to the more advanced organisms (especially human beings), life and experience have analogies all the way down to the sub-atomic level and all the way up to God. I am a panpsychist in a broadly Whiteheadian sense. See Alfred North Whitehead, *Process and Reality*, Corrected Edition, ed. by David Ray Griffin and Donald W. Sherburne (New York: Free Press, 1978). See my *Theological Biology*, 207-24.

7. Evil and suffering arise only when being is disordered or injured; i. e, its proper structure is disrupted or partially destroyed or rendered dysfunctional. Goodness is a quality of being in so far as it is being, i. e., embodies its own proper determinate form and fulfills its potential. For whom is it good? The answer is some experiencing subject acknowledging (a) the intrinsic goodness of ones own existence, (b) the intrinsic goodness of another experiencing subject, or the instrumental good of some being in relation to some purpose.

8. The Uncreated suggests that the ultimate factors that account for the becoming that produced our actual world are eternal. Yet it is no more difficult for me to imagine that the Uncreated factors arose contingently and spontaneously from (presumably) "nothing" as to conceive that they are eternal and necessary. In any case, the Uncreated refers to the ultimate, self-existent elements that account for everything else, whether they are emergent and contingent or eternal and necessary. I propose the Uncreated to specify what might ultimately underlie the presently actual world as its source and ground but which is not dependent on anything prior to itself. It is a hypothesis based on an intuition about the nature of the process of becoming itself.

9. Three decades ago I speculated that the ultimate factors were nothing, the possible, the actual, and the ideal (the good), describing the creative process observed in the cosmos as the possible becoming actual under the lure of the good, thus creating the new from what originally was nothing. I professed agnosticism regarding the relationship among them in the Uncreated. Here I assume but do not include nothing and substitute Eros for the actual. I conjecture that Eros is the dynamic, creative, powerful capacity to originate from nothing the simplest actuality possible, either space-time or some more elementary emergent. While these three factors can be distinguished abstractly with respect to the distinctive character of each, neither is fully what it is apart from its interaction with the others. They are apposites who require each other for completion. See my *Science, Secularization and God* (Nashville: Abingdon Press, 1969), 146-94

10. To put it differently, "a possibility is an available structure for some process of actualization. To become is to take on some determinate form, to move toward being something definite." *Science, Secularization and God*, 156. I am doubtful of the existence of a realm of timeless forms (Plato) or eternal objects (Whitehead) for all the reasons that critics have raised over the centuries. It boggles the mind to think that there is a discrete, particular form for every entity or circumstance that exists or that conceivably could exist. How many eternal objects are there to represent all the possible shades of blue? Perhaps, as Charles Hartshorne once suggested,

it is better to resort to the vague notion of an indeterminate, continuous, general realm or matrix or fund of possibility inclusive of whatever can be from which discrete, particular forms of definiteness emerge descriptive of whatever in fact comes to pass. R. G. Collingwood shows the opposite difficulties that Samuel Alexander and A. N. Whitehead fall into because the former does not while the latter has a doctrine of an eternal realm of possibility. See *The Idea of Nature* (New York: Oxford Galaxy Book, 1960), 161-5, 171-3.

11. Good has many meanings. In addition to being what which properly satisfies Eros, the Good can be seen "as (1) the value-quality coincident with organic actualization, as (2) that which is instrumental to the achievement of (3) an ideal toward which process or a developing organism is driven and drawn." *Science, Secularization and God*, 157. My idea of the relationship between Possibility and The Good is akin to that in Plato's thought between the Forms and The Good. Alfred North Whitehead is a primary 20th century mentor, although by beginning with the elementary and proceeding to the more advanced, my outlook is much indebted to Samuel Alexander, *Space, Time, and Deity*, 2 vols. (New York: The Macmillan Co., 1920). My theory of value (the good) owes much to Henry Nelson Wieman, *The Source of Human Good* (Chicago: University of Chicago Press, 1946).

12. Whether space-time is primordial and uncreated or among the first creations I do not know. If so, it would constitute a fourth constituent of the Uncreated, a primitive form of actuality. Here I assume that space-time is an early and elementary emergent.

13. In this respect, I agree with Bernard Loomer, "The Size of God," in *The Size of God: The Theology of Bernard Loomer in Context*, ed. by William Dean and Larry Axel (Macon: Mercer University Press, 1987), 20-51. If there are structural factors within the world that in some sense underlie or at least account for its particular processive, evolving character, then Loomer's position and mine may not much different.

14. Shailer Mathews, *The Growth of the Idea of God* (New York: The Macmillan Co., 1931), 210-34.

15. Cf. Charles Hartshorne, *A Natural Theology for Our Time* (LaSalle: Open Court Publishing Co., 1967), 5-12, 34-41, 136.

16. Scientists will not discover this element in their investigations, since their methods are not equipped to detect it. Eros and the good are terms descriptive of the character of organisms as a whole and of the processes by which they actualize their potential. I have argued in several places against a "scientism" that presupposes that only what science can discover is real. I reject mechanistic reductionism that to seeks explanations

for all phenomena associated with organisms in terms of physics and chemistry. I hold with Whitehead that science provides us with only half the evidence, namely what can be discovered by observing entities from the outside, neglecting what is experienced by organisms from the inside. I hold to a strong organicism that stops short of becoming vitalism. For a discussion of these ideas, see my *Science, Secularization and God*, 53-61, 94-130; and *Theological Biology*, 65-120, 184-231.

17. Alfred North Whitehead, *The Function of Reason* (Princeton: Princeton University Press, 1929), 8.

18. I have attempted to state similar views on these subjects in more detail in a previous work. See Cauthen, *Science, Secularization and God*, 90-130, 146-58, 161-81.

19. For a brief discussion, see my *Systematic Theology* (Lewiston: Edwin Mellen Press, 1986), 87-93.

20. For an illuminating discussion of the complexities, similarities, and differences between metaphor and symbol, see Paul Ricouer, *Interpretation Theory* (Fort Worth: Texas Christian University Press, 1976), 45-69. For a more detailed study of the history and meaning of metaphor, see his *The Rule of Metaphor* (Toronto: University of Toronto Press, 1977). For a technical analysis of the different kinds of language about God, see Schubert Ogden, *The Point of Christology* (New York: Harper & Row, 1982), 131-47.

21. Here my position is closely related to that of Paul Tillich. See *Systematic Theology*, I:263-67.

22. Here my position is close to that of Gordon Kaufman, who distinguishes between the "master act of God" that is accomplished in the whole of the cosmos and human history and "sub-acts" that as stages along the way contribute to the fulfillment of the "master act." See "On the Meaning of `Act of God,'" in Owen Thomas, ed., *God's Activity in the World* (Chico, CA: Scholars Press, 1983), 137-61.

23. Another distinction important for a thorough consideration of evil is that between absolute and relative evil. Absolute evil is suffering that is pointless, unnecessary, purely destructive with no redeeming elements or outcomes for anyone ever. Relative evil is suffering that is partially, wholly, or more than compensated for in some larger context or in the long run.

24. I have developed these themes in detail in a forthcoming book under the title *The Many Faces of Evil: Reflections on the Sinful, the Tragic, the Demonic, and the Ambigous*.

25. One can locate errors of reasoning in the defense of various positions. Some might be so fundamental as to negate the proposition itself, but no theory can be established positively as most assuredly and certainly

true.

26. I have argued these points in detail before. See my *Science, Secularization and God*, 170-81. In that work I argued for the postulation of a "dark impediment," a flaw in the divine perfection that accounted for some of the absurd evil in the world. While not repudiating that notion, I now more frankly adopt the view of a finite, opportunistic God perfect in intention but limited in power who struggles to actualize the potential for good in the cosmos in an adventure filled with an ambiguous intertwining of good and evil. My present views are closer to those found in my *Theological Biology*, 121-75.

27. I have defined the good life, the good person, the good society, justice, happiness, and enjoyment in a series of works over two decades. See *Science, Secularization and God*, 227-8; *Christian Biopolitics* (Nashville: Abingdon Press, 1971), 103-53; *The Ethics of Enjoyment* (Atlanta: John Knox Press, 1975), 64-100; *Process Ethics* (Lewiston: Edwin Mellen Press, 1984), 37-82, 125-315; and *The Passion for Equality* (Totowa, NJ: Rowman & Littlefield, 1987), 1-30, 63-177.

28. See Shailer Mathews, *The Growth of the Idea of God*.

29. In other words, I accept as "canons of historical inquiry" the principles of homogeneity and analogy. All events of the past and future exhibit the same patterns and possibilities, and events in the past must be interpreted as analogous to events that occur in the present. In this respect I am in complete agreement with Whitehead that an interpretation of history rests on experience in the here and now. See *Religion in the Making* (New York: The Macmillan Co., 1926), 82. Cf. my *Science, Secularization and God*, 198-200. Hence, I disagree with Barth, whose confidence in revelation allows him to ignore or by-pass scientific understandings of nature based on ordinary secular experience that would preclude virgin births and bodily resurrections. See *Church Dogmatics*, 4 vols. (Edinburgh: T & T Clark, 1936-69) I, 2:172-202; III, 2:439-55; IV, 1:341. I also disagree with Wolfhart Pannenberg, who thinks that one can rationally prove the resurrection of Jesus. Proof is a function of perspective. It is based on a network of assumptions internal to the total outlook within which particular claims are made. Pannenberg can prove that the resurrection was an objective historical event only to those who share his more general assumptions about how we know and what we know. It would be foolish for him to claim that those who disagree with him are irrational or incompetent. All interpretations of such complicated matters are relative, and no universality can be claimed for them. Specifically, Pannenberg could not give credence to the evidence that the resurrection is a unique event unless he were already prepared *on other grounds* to conceive the possibility of such an

event. One might argue that the evidence for some events is so powerful and irresistible that it may destroy previous belief in their non-possibility and force acceptance of their possibility on the basis of their actuality. However, it is difficult to see how the evidence for the resurrection can be of this paradigm-shaking sort. The evidence is limited, second hand, difficult to assess, and other explanations are readily available that adequately account for the data. See *Basic Questions*, 2 vols. (Philadelphia: Westminster Press, 1970-1), I, chapter 2. For a similar view, see Jürgen Moltmann, *Theology of Hope* (New York: Harper & Row, 1967), 172-90. In this respect I agree with Langdon Gilkey. See his brief but succinct analysis of the philosophical issues in *Naming the Whirlwind* (Indianapolis: Bobbs-Merrill, 1970), 361n35. The neo-orthodox are right in claiming that belief in the possibility of the resurrection is a "faith judgment." It only needs to be added that disbelief in the possibility and actuality of the resurrection of Christ as a supernatural cosmic event is also a "faith judgment," where faith means not the response to a supernatural revelation but a particular intellectual perspective not susceptible of rational demonstration to all competent and unbiased persons. Skeptics and believers all live by faith in this sense.

30. This gets to be quite a subtle point. One might argue that one of the general principles operating in the world is that exceptional events are possible. One could further assert that if one believes in an omnipotent God whose will determines all things, the possibility of exceptional events is a reasonable principle. Hence, if Jesus were born of a virgin or were raised from the dead, this would be an exceptional event in that virgins do not generally give birth and the dead generally are not raised. Yet these events would violate no general principle, since one general principle is that exceptions can occur. Whether they have occurred is a matter for inquiry and debate. One might then argue that the virgin birth and/or the resurrection of Jesus actually did occur based on the evidence presented by the Scriptures as a reliable witness. Obviously I am denying both the possibility of radical contingency as a general principle operating in nature and history and the fact of radical contingency with respect to particular occurrences. If one has sufficient grounds for assuming the existence of a free, transcendent, almighty Lord or for establishing the Scriptures as a witness whose claims cannot be contravened in a system of thought in which all these assumptions and beliefs cohere and are mutually supportive, then one has a sufficient basis for entertaining both the possibility and the actuality of the virgin birth and the resurrection of Jesus, along with any other miracles that are supported by Scripture or experience.

Since my theology rests on principles that are derived from present experience, I have no grounds for assuming either the incontrovertible veracity of Scripture or the reality of an omnipotent divine will. Moreover, the human experience available to me first hand provides no grounds for the assertion of radical contingency either as a possibility or as a necessity. No exceptional events in the required sense in question here have occurred in my experience or in the experience of many others whose witness I trust most. Yet I must be cautious here, since the evolutionary process does give rise to the new and to the unexpected. Yet the mutations that produce new species spring from potentialities that emerge gradually over the course of time and do not exemplify the kind of radical contingency that miracles in the old-fashioned sense call for.

I need not repeat the argument that debates about such matters as complicated as this admit of no universal or certain resolution. We are all finally grasped by a *Gestalt* that we cannot deny and to which we must give witness.

31. Reinhold Niebuhr, *Faith and History* (New York: Charles Scribner's Sons, 1949); Loomer, "The Size of God."

32. This includes not only medical discoveries that control pain and disease but other technologies that improve the human lot and make life easier. In the social and moral sphere as well, the rise of democratic ideals and doctrines of human rights based on the liberty and equality of all persons represent an advance over notions of the divine rights of kings and other doctrines that justified non-consensual government. Certainly the lot of blacks, women, and Native Americans in this country shows improvement over the last century and a half, although much remains in current practice that is scandalous to justice. In some respects both moral ideals and moral practice move upward. In the 19th century learned persons defended slavery and opposed suffrage for women. They used both Scripture and natural law to justify prevailing customs. No one who did so today would be taken seriously. Yet the murder of six million Jews by a highly educated, supposedly advanced nation is a twentieth century phenomena. Cruelty, violence, terrorism, and oppression are still widespread sponsored by states as well as by individuals. The fact that hunger, disease, and poverty that could be prevented are still the lot of millions of people at this very hour gives us reason to be cautious about making claims regarding the advance of moral practice. Moreover, the possibility of ecological disaster during the next century casts doubt on the ability of human beings to act wisely and sufficiently in time to counteract the increasing hazards produced by the very technology that was supposed to emancipate us.

33. See my *Systematic Theology*, 392-8; and Gilkey, *Naming the Whirlwind*, 226-38.

34. See Tillich, *The Protestant Era* (Chicago: University of Chicago Press, 1948), xvii-xxi. See also his *The Interpretation of History* (New York: Charles Scribner's Sons, 1936).

35. A recent work on the economy provides an illustration. After a prediction of wide-spread joblessness in the future, Stanley Aronowitz and William DiFazio urge policies that they recognize are politically impossible to achieve in the present. Their argument is that it is useful for some to explore alternatives that would be effective even though they are not feasible in the current political climate. In my terms, they go beyond *realistic hope* while remaining pretty far short of *utopian hope*. See their *The Jobless Future: Sci-Tech and the Dogma of Work* (Minneapolis: University of Minnesota Press, 1994), 328-58.

36. When a loved one dies, the context must be widened so that the living who remain can seek meaning and enjoyment in their own lives from that day forward. For those about to die and for loving family surrounding them, the context must be narrowed so that what it is hoped for it is not deliverance from death but that whatever possibilities of physical comfort and human companionship arise from day to day can be realized before death opens up the wider context.

Chapter Six

Christ and Christians

"No idea is so outlandish that it should not be considered with a searching, but at the same time with a steady, eye".[1]

In a student's term paper handed me recently, it was stated that Jesus thought of God as Mother, Lover, and Friend, the familiar metaphors employed by Sallie McFague.[2] This prompted an overly long response from the professor urging caution in finding too close an identity between Jesus' theology and ours. The instructor went to acknowledge that the student was following a long and more or less honorable tradition.

Everyone who has thought about it surely must be struck with how Jesus is remade in every theology to fit the image that particular outlook requires. I mean to imply more than mere harmony between the description of Jesus viewed as the Christ and the rest of that particular theology. In any good perspective, this concord will, of course, obtain. I want further to insist that the interpreter gives the final shape both to the theology as a whole and to the person and work of Christ within that framework. The Christ Christians believe in is constructed by them (or by the tradition they uphold), but the assumption generally is that the real Jesus of Nazareth corresponds to that particular description. Put otherwise, the underlying premise is that one examines the normative sources and perhaps the experience of Christians in order to discover the person and nature of Jesus as Christ. The interpreting subject (the believer) comes to know the object (Christ) while functioning as a transparent medium through which the reality is captured in appropriate concepts. The resulting portrait is assumed to be descriptive of the reality as it is in itself. Certainly this was the way the formulators of the classical creeds saw their task. The Reformers viewed themselves as continuing the objectivist tradition of Chalcedon, and so did the theologians of Protestant orthodoxy. The search for the historical Jesus in the 19th century was an attempt by critical historical study to discover the actual person behind the creeds and the Christologies. The historian replaced the metaphysician as the author of the real truth about the central figure of the faith.

In the 20th century theologians seriously affected by the corrosive acids of relativity and pluralism have been more circumspect about their claims regarding the correspondence between the Jesus Christ of their theologies and the biblical Christ who lived long ago. Yet if one picks up a theological text, whether a systematic theology or a monograph on Christology, one usually gets the impression that the authors are not just articulating their own vision of Jesus as Christ but are describing a reality objective to them who was in fact much like the picture they have painted of him. When pressed, of course, the authors may give their own disquisition on historical relativism, opt for pluralism, and settle for modest claims regarding the correspondence between their Christology and the Christ of history. The end result, however, is not to abandon the connection between the depicted Christ and the real one who taught beside the Sea but only to qualify it variously. One is generally left with the impression that the author is pretty sure it is the factual Jesus who is the final sanction for the beliefs and values espoused as authoritative for today.

To pursue the theme further, consider a couple of examples. David Griffin asserts that Jesus fully and consistently appropriated as his subjective aim the initial aim provided by God for his life under circumstances that produced a special revelation of the character and purpose of God. How are we to understand that?[3] Is Griffin suggesting merely that if we were to ask how Jesus might be interpreted by a theologian who has adopted the metaphysics of Alfred North Whitehead, this is how it might come out? Is he saying only that this is a useful way for him to think about Jesus and that he offers that possibility for our consideration -- assuming, of course, that we could first be converted to Whiteheadianism? Or is he saying that in fact God proffered ideal possibilities or normative aims moment to moment to the growing Jesus and that Jesus both fully ascertained these aims and fully adopted them as his own? Does he believe that God actually has a primordial nature with the features described by Whitehead? Is he offering his view of Jesus as truth corresponding to reality that we at last in the 20th century have been fortunate to come across thanks to the great philosopher? When Paul Tillich maintains that Jesus exhibits a union of essence and existence under the conditions of existence, do these categories capture reality as it objectively is?[4] Or is this simply a useful way to view Jesus in the light of the metaphysics of Paul Tillich? Did Tillich discover essence and existence as veridical categories objectively present in the real Jesus, or did he invent (or better adopt) them as helpful ways of interpreting the New Testament witness? If Griffin and Tillich are literalists about their categories in relation to reality, in what sense can they both be right? They are in formal agreement, of course, in teaching that Jesus was the ideal human being whose person and work constitute a normative disclosure of God. Both are wrong, of course, as measured by Chalcedonian dogma, since neither Griffin nor Tillich thinks that Jesus was literally God in one of his natures. If all three are to be taken in terms of whether their theories correspond to reality, we have to make a choice as to which, if either, meets the test.

AN ALTERNATIVE PROPOSAL

I want to propose a thesis that bypasses these questions. Christians, or the traditions in which they stand, are the authors of their Christologies and the main correspondence is with the theological systems in which they appear and with the overall belief systems of the various authors. Every portrait of Christ is relative to the cultural context of the theologians who paint them. Each one reflects a view of reality as a whole along with an understanding of what humans beings need to achieve the ideal life. The Jesus depicted in these multitudinous Christologies undoubtedly has some connection with the facts of history, including the message, ministry, and intentions of the man himself. The connection, however, cannot be precisely known with certainty.

The problem is that we cannot compare our Christologies with the real Christ to discern where they do and do not accurately portray the past in adequate language. We cannot make that comparison because every Christ available to us is already an interpretation of the reality we wish to encounter and not merely the reality itself. Each of the Gospels presents its own particular slant on Jesus. The Jesus who spoke as he is represented as doing in John did not likely speak as he is said to in the other three. The best we can do is to use these original portraits to measure our own, but this opens a very wide door. Before we can proceed, we have to adopt a procedure for studying and interpreting the Gospels. Any method we might adopt carries with it presuppositions about how historical documents are to be studied. Finally, when we ask what Christ requires of us today, the role of the contemporary interpreter becomes even more prominent, even decisive.

It may be thought that I am here neglecting the role of Christian experience in providing data relevant to the formulation of a doctrine of Christ. That is not my intention. Indeed, my own view is that the meaning of Jesus for faith does ultimately rest on the way in which the encounter with Scripture and the impact of that remarkable life and ministry enter into the determination of how we think, feel, and act with respect to fundamental religious and moral matters. Nevertheless, experience, like the Bible, must be interpreted. My point is, as always, that the role of the interpreter is definitive.

The implications of this way of understanding Christologies lead me to a form of pragmatism in which the terms of the argument are thoroughly recast. The definitive question ceases to be whether the Christ of our Christologies corresponds with the Christ of history. The compelling issue is whether one has dealt with the historical materials as responsibly as possible to construct a model of Jesus as the Christ that (1) has salvific functions within a framework shaped by that Christian's or that tradition's belief system and (2) is congruent with it as a whole. The final test, then, is whether the resulting picture of the Christ present in Jesus is harmonious with the rest of one's beliefs and whether it functions to promote the highest ends of life for oneself and others, specifically unity with God and neighbor.

Conflicting Christologies will still confront one another in abundance. However, we would evaluate them not by their correspondence with the past but by their power to promote the best possible life here and now. That judgment is made in light of the best that we know up to know from all sources about everything relevant to the issues at hand. The consequence is that we speak of Jesus the Christ as he is known by us in our lives and in our theologies without making any definitive claims about the identity of our Jesus with the actual Jesus of the past. The Jesus known to us as the normative Christ doubtless has connections, even points of identity, with the Jesus of history.

However, since we cannot sort out the truth and the falsity of the various components of our picture of the historical Jesus Christ, we cannot make the historical truthfulness of our portraits the necessary underpinning of our own normative beliefs about the means and ends of the ideal life. Did Jesus hold an apocalyptic view of the full manifestation of the Realm of God? I dare not rely on the answers of the historians for anything terribly important to present faith since the next generation of scholars now writing dissertations in Cambridge or Claremont or Heidelberg or somewhere will undermine the foundations. Beliefs about reality and morality must justify themselves in experience here and now as critically interpreted by reason in light of what we cannot help but believe about the world, its creative Source, and its possibilities for affording the good life for the citizens of planet earth.[5]

JESUS AND HIS INTERPRETERS

With this general survey of the territory I wish to explore in mind, let me proceed more systematically. Who can ever forget those words of George Tyrell about the picture of Jesus that Adolf Harnack set before us as the genuine article. Harnack, said Tyrell, looked deeply into the well of history to see what was on the bottom. When the water got still and the features of Jesus became visible, he saw "only the reflection of a liberal Protestant face."[6] We laugh at poor Harnack who made Jesus over in his own image, who saw his own visage at the bottom of the well. Our glee should make us nervous. Alas, what holds for Adolf Harnack pertains to us all!

The Marxist Jesus is a social radical calling the masses of the oppressed to revolution. In a book that claims to offer "a discovery of the real Jesus," Bruce Barton insists that Jesus had a business man's mentality.[7] For feminists, Jesus held equalitarian ideals free from any bias of gender. For liberation theology, he is a here and now liberator of the socially oppressed. For the Baptists I grew up with, Jesus bore the wrath of God on the cross so we could be forgiven and go to heaven. For slave holders Jesus told approving stories about slave owners and thus implicitly sanctioned slavery (Matthew 25:14ff NRSV). The Ku Klux Klan uses a burning cross as its symbol. We could make this list as long as we wanted. Christians have countenanced nearly every evil and supported just about every good (by somebody's assessment) cause imaginable. All have claimed Jesus to be the authoritative source of their doctrines and practices.

What biblical scholars in succeeding generations affirm Jesus to have taught about the Realm of God neatly coincides with the requirements of theological movements that rise and fall. Compare Adolf Harnack and Rudolf Bultmann.[8] The former's idealistic teacher contrasts neatly with the latter's existentialist preacher. The immanent God of the 19th century liberals and the transcendent God of the 20th century neo-orthodox took turns being the real, the only, God that Jesus knew. It seems Jesus can be whoever and whatever we want, need, and sincerely believe him to be.

When I was in seminary in the 1950's, we knew that the old search for the Jesus of history was bankrupt. The synoptic Gospels are not biographies, the reasoning went, but theological portraits. We had always known this was true of the Gospel of John. Now it seemed Mark, Matthew, and Luke were theologians too, setting forth the meaning of Jesus for their faith. They, of course, had slightly different theologies, so their pictures of Jesus corresponded as required. The rejection of "The Quest" was soon followed by a "New Quest."[9] Whatever the consensus may be at the moment, if there is one, in the leading centers of inquiry, it will be followed by new proposals that will have their fifteen minutes of scholarly fame.[10]

The project of "The Jesus Seminar," conducted by Robert W. Funk and other high-profile scholars, was to give us a judgment on which of the reported words in the Gospels were actually uttered by Jesus.[11] Does anybody seriously think this can be done in a way that will justify enough confidence in the results to do anything important with them? One may, of course, use the conclusions for practical purposes, but surely one must do so with great tentativeness, since next years's investigations may lead to conflicting conclusions. The Seminar scholars certainly did not -- could not -- settle the issue once and for all. Is it important for theology and faith to get answers to Seminar questions? Or are these efforts worthwhile only to record history correctly, even in this tentative, uncertain, problematic fashion? If the latter, I certainly would not quarrel with the aspiration. Many will doubt both the wisdom and the efficacy of the enterprise. Others will criticize the methods and assumptions employed, while also refuting the conclusions of the investigators. That the results can be helpful to me as a contemporary person in quest of help with living, I doubt. An exception to this judgment would occur, of course, if historical investigation into what Jesus said or did unearthed novel insights hitherto undiscovered that illuminated the nature of human existence and its ideal possibilities. But it would be the convincing insight that was useful not the fact that it originated with Jesus. It is the value of the words for faith that matters, not whether Jesus did or did not say them.

Yet while many will recognize that in every theology Jesus is pictured as being exactly what he needs to be to constitute the authoritative basis for that particular perspective, few seem to draw from that fact the conclusions that I now find compelling. The problem, of course, is that these theological outlooks, each with a portrait of Jesus favorable to itself, contradict each other to one degree or another, approaching total mutual annihilation at the extremes. This plain fact does not seem to produce the trepidation in others that it arouses in me. One outlook may be in fact true and the others false, but which one, and in what sense is it true? Any attempt to unravel these issues will hurl us headlong into the briar patch of epistemological inquiry, long the burying ground of profitable discourse.[12] Nevertheless, the mission demands a brief rehearsal of options.[13]

KNOWING THE REAL JESUS

We can distinguish between two polar extremes. I will propose a third way, but one that is not found as a point on the continuum between the opposite poles. I should acknowledge that I am not alone in affirming the third option.

THE REALISTS

At one extreme are the realists, who assert that we can have reliable knowledge of the objectively real. Two versions of this are current.

(1) Absolutists

At the polar extreme of realism are the absolutists. Put simply, there is a truth that corresponds with reality, and they are in full, total, and exclusive possession of it. Adherents to this rendering of things can with confidence pronounce views that deviate from their own as purely and simply wrong. They know that they have come to a knowledge of the real, the one and only Jesus. Readers may fill in this category with their favorite representatives of dogmatic fervor.

(2) Critical Realists

More modest are the critical realists, who have been contaminated with various degrees of historical relativism. Since I am a former or recovering adherent, let me describe my version. Reality is "out there," and truth faithful to its features can partially and perhaps even progressively be attained. At least our depictions of matters historical and ontological can be held with enough confidence for us to proceed practically to work out the implications for belief and behavior. Critical realists constitute a broad spectrum, varying among themselves in part on how far away they are from the absolutists as determined by how fully and in what form they embrace relativism. Generally, they speak of a Jesus who is real to them and are sure that their theological version of him is valid, but not exclusively so. They are tolerant pluralists who must admit into the household of faith a variety of Christologies (though doubtless ruling out the most abhorrent as plainly spurious), even though it is impossible to reconcile them all.

It is not easy to make a neat classification of contemporary theologians with respect to their realism, but some widespread themes can be noted.[14] Relativity and pluralism are commonly accepted. The literature reveals an agonizing quest for universal truths while fully recognizing that justification of belief occurs within particular communities that both devise the warrants and conduct the testing, producing a obdurate multitude of conflicting perspectives. A yearning for a public theology based on general rational principles is frustrated by the lack of consensus in church and society regarding what constitutes right reasoning about the big questions. The constructive character of theology is widely recognized. Theological perspectives are relative, tentative, partial attempts to grasp the reality of God and to formulate doctrines of

Christ. Tentative, relative adequacy is the most that can be claimed for our efforts. Conversation is urged among representatives of different and conflicting outlooks with an openness to appropriate insights from each other so that commonality may grow. Mutual creative transformation may occur in these encounters. Without surrendering the idea of a reality referent, correspondence may be redefined to mean a consensus of well-grounded belief.[15] Moreover, a practical test in terms of the efficacy of an outlook to provide understanding and to facilitate justice and human fulfillment is urged by many.

Critical realism is nuanced in a multitude of ways that tilt in some versions toward a kind of confidence in theory that moves toward absolutism and leans in others in the direction of deconstruction and pragmatism. Nearly all move between the poles of a hopeful craving for universal truth accessible to all and the recognition that beliefs are generated and justified within particular frames of reference in a situation where no supreme court is available to settle stubbornly persisting disputes. No one has been able to find a way "beyond objectivism and relativism" that is itself not quickly refuted by other candidates for the job.[16]

THE DECONSTRUCTIONISTS

At the other extreme opposite the absolutist realists is deconstruction.[17] If anyone goes all the way to the end in undialectical fashion, we find the startling denial that our writing about God and Jesus is about reality.[18] Every theory expressed in words is just one more in a never ending series of interpretations. There is no truth about objective reality, only points of view, no knowledge, only opinions. We write and we speak, but we do so with respect to other speaking and writing. Never does the reference transcend the text itself but is always to other texts.[19] Interpretation is of other interpretations and rests on interpretations all the way down and all the way across. There are no fixed or right meanings and no text-transcending realities in our witness that can be properly known and accurately described. There is only the text itself; neither author nor referent matter.

Deconstruction functions within a postmodern framework defined by Cornel West as "anti-foundational, anti-totalizing, and demystifying."[20] No foundation can be found upon which to erect indubitable structures of truth. Theories that try to explain everything in one all-encompassing scheme are rejected. Systems of ideas and ideals are infected with ideologies that further self-interest and justify the possession of dominating power. Widely quoted is Jean François Lyotard, "Simplifying to the extreme, I define "postmodern" as incredulity toward metanarratives."[21] A metanarrative is the big story being worked out in all the little stories, the overarching pattern and direction exhibited in the many particular events of history.

Deconstruction rejects "the metaphysics of presence" associated with "logocentric" (Derrida) schemes that purport to capture reality in dependable structures of rational doctrine. Likewise, it abhors binary oppositions in which one term of the pair is favored over the other, whereas we are urged to embrace and appreciate difference in dialectical interplay with identity. Seldom is anything presented unparadoxically, unambiguously, or unequivocally. All is an endless artistic play of dialectical moments and movements in which nothing is ever just simply what it is. Does deconstruction completely deny or disregard the connection between language and reality? In some versions it seems to.[22] In any case, at the end of the road down which deconstruction starts lies an extreme point at which talk and text are totally severed from any pretensions of grasping the objectively real.

Within this framework, one can play with various interpretations of Jesus or the Word become words in texts and find some of them useful for some purposes as long as one does not pin anything down tightly, permanently, or simply.[23] Given its transgressive character in which established rules of academic scholarship are questioned and in which no hermeneutical scheme is privileged or foundational, what then are to be the criteria by which we measure deconstructionist exegesis and theology? It would appear to me that pragmatic tests might be the best way to go, but doubtless that would be altogether too confining, too constricted, an attempt to stop the interminable succession of reinterpreted interpretations. If not pragmatism, what? My suspicion is that the most extreme among them take aesthetic delight in pleasuring themselves with dangerous thrills by flirting with a latent and lurking intellectual nihilism, but never undialectically, of course. Yet the theologians seem genuinely troubled in their joy that God, self, history, and the Bible are all dead, but not in any final or total way.[24] One deals with presence in absence and absence in presence, and negation gets negated in an endless serpentine interplay of opposites with no beginnings, middles, or endings. We begin where we happen to be and do the best we can with what we have around the margins groping and grasping never content with any conclusion for long in a continuing process in which answers become new questions, and opposites become each other.[25]

Deconstruction, moderate or extreme, is one option for critical realists so overwhelmed by relativism, pluralism, and uncertainty that it appears to be the only recourse.[26] Along with the surprising, astonishing, and unsettling but edifying insights its adventurous explorations might produce, its main value is negative. It exploits the follies of the absolutists and the inherent ambiguities of the critical realists who think they are in touch with reality but who cannot be certain about what is true and false in their interpretations. Pluralism within a realist context is unstable and is tempted either to resolve its anxieties by creeping closer toward some new confident scheme or by wandering near the pit of nihilism in the company of the furthest out representatives of deconstruction. To put it differently, critical reason infected with relativism generates a tolerant pluralism that founders on the rock of uncertainty. It can neither pronounce its opponents wrong or claim that ones own view is thoroughly true. Yet I prefer critical realism to deconstruction, but my version slides over into pragmatism.

PRAGMATISM

Pragmatism does not position itself at some point on the continuum between the realists and the deconstructionists but reframes the problem and sets it into a quite different context. On the basis of realism, once you accept the full consequence of relativism and pluralism, you simply cannot be certain about the truthfulness of your own views, where truth means correspondence with reality. Moreover, unless all the competing versions, which in confrontation range from the mildly incompatible to the utterly irreconcilable, can all be equally true, i. e., descriptive of reality, then all but one outlook is at least partially false anyway. But which file contains the true one, and how can I download it to my system? But, the argument goes, we can claim to have partial correspondence with reality or a valid perspective. The problem is that you have no way of judging what are the correct and the incorrect aspects of your assertions since you cannot compare your interpretation with the reality as it is in itself. How do you know if you have partial knowledge if you cannot compare the part with the whole? And if you can discern the whole, knowledge need not be partial or only a perspective. If you can know reality as it is, you can just describe it, i. e., produce an interpretation that corresponds with it. Reinterpreting the correspondence theory of truth to mean "the consensus of warranted beliefs" is a good move but does not resolve the basis tension between the craving of universality and the recognition of the historicity and relativity of thought. Defining the criteria of beliefs that are "warranted" calls for the elaboration of principles that remain in interminable dispute.

The central problem is that we cannot compare our theories with the uninterpreted real Jesus to determine how close we are to the mark. One other little troublesome question has to do with what we take "the real Jesus" to mean and refer to. There is no Jesus except an interpreted one. I agree that the interpretations intend to be interpretations of the real. However, we cannot adjudicate our conflicting perspectives except within some framework of common assumptions. Unfortunately, since competing sets of underlying assumptions are themselves in dispute and cannot be conclusively established with guaranteed results, we are adrift in a morass of irresolvable controversies. Here I seem to be slipping into deconstruction. I escape by reframing the question so that the alternatives do not run between realism and deconstruction.

Continuing meditation on the changing, conflicting currents of scholarship and reflection convinced me gradually that my trust in realism, no matter how critical, was misplaced. How could the particular stage or version of things that compelled my acceptance be worthy of bearing the weight I had put upon it? As I have reviewed the course of biblical and theological developments over the decades, I have increasingly become a skeptic, a more pronounced relativist, and a pragmatist.

In the background is an assumption that guides what I am about to say. Three points of reference are relevant to knowledge: reality, experience, and interpretation.[27] The problem is that we can never sort these elements out infallibly. Each depends on the others. Neither can be defined without reference to the other two. They are indissolubly connected to each other. Our schemes, we may claim, are interpretations of reality based on our experience. But there is no reality (for us) apart from our experience of it, and our experience of reality is always interpreted. We always deal with experienced reality as interpreted or interpreted reality as experienced or interpreted experiences of reality.

Given this assumption, my proposal is that the frame of reference must not be whether theories correspond to the objects theorized about. The test must be in terms of whether a theory is harmonious with the whole set of convictions we find compelling based on the best we know from all sources up to now. The frame of reference is our experienced world. In our experience we engage a world objective to us and real in its own terms, but we can only speak of reality as it is experienced by us. The world is what it is experienced to be. Or as William James said, reality is what it is "known as."[28] By referring to what is real for us in experience we can create and test interpretations that prove themselves by making sense of our experienced world. Moreover, we can organize vast amounts of data into highly complex networks of mutually supporting and reinforcing theories that ideally approach as a (surely unattainable) goal a total interpretation of experienced reality. Theories can be revised or abandoned as need be. The tests are two: (1) The *empirical* test is whether a point of view adequately accounts for all available relevant evidence. (2) The *rational* test is whether a theory fits harmoniously with the rest of our presently held beliefs and values. Success is partial; theories must be held tentatively, ever open to revision in light of better evidence or more acute reasoning.

I believe certain advantages accrue to regarding the message, meaning, ministry, and intention of Jesus, as well as the symbols of incarnation and resurrection, in this framework. We can have a basis for our own faith and practice without having to argue with others about who has the truth that corresponds to the reality. Christians with competing views of the Christ can debate each other vigorously. The grounds for holding to a certain outlook can be specified and defended. More important that the content of the arguments themselves may be the recitation of the history that led to their being regarded as decisive. Most views will reveal areas of common agreement with others. Usually the circles of interpretation will overlap to varying degrees. Seldom will they lie totally outside each other. Interpretations can be revised, defended, or abandoned by all parties as their advocates find it necessary within their own terms or as their larger assumptions may get undermined or reframed.

It is true that in the end when all the argument is done, each must say, "It works for me, but I cannot specify to what degree and in what respect my views mirror the objective reality of Jesus believed in as the Christ." Final testing is made in terms of pragmatic efficacy and not in terms of correspondence with reality.[29] Pragmatic efficacy means that a view provides understanding of the world for me within my frame of reference, and it provides me with routines of practice that facilitate coping with life's challenges and that promote the highest ends of life as I have come to discern them experimentally and experientially. With William James we may ask what practical difference it makes in real life whether we hold one doctrine or another. If there is no discernible dissimilarity in experience or in the implications for behavior, disputes may be safely ignored or left unresolved.[30] Interpretive schemes and routines of habits and practices are subject to revision in the light of compelling experiential evidence and rational argument.

When pictures of Jesus and formal Christologies are viewed in this way, we will not be surprised at the variety of them and at their conflicting conclusions. Neither need we worry about which correspond to reality most fully. That question cannot be settled except by sheer declaration. Nor need we be anxious about whether our own images of Jesus with their implications for living are authentic expressions that Jesus himself would approve. We can only say that our views of Jesus represent the best we know using the best sources and most convincing interpretive frameworks available to us so far. I can compare my views with others, knowing that I am comparing *my views* with *other views*. I can be influenced by them, or I can reject them. I can ask if my views are consistent with available evidence, if they fit with the rest of my beliefs, and if they are useful in guiding me and others to a better, happier, more loving, more just world, as I judge these matters.

The standard objection to this kind of pragmatism is that it lands us in a relativism in which anything goes that works for someone. If relativism means that everybody's beliefs are as good as anybody else's or that no system of values is any better than another, perhaps we should worry -- if anybody could be found who actually believed that and lived by it.[31] If relativism means that the only way to justify claims is to make use of the resources available to us in our own time and place, surely a good case can be made for the doctrine.[32] Remaining to be resolved is what is required in the way of belief essential to discovering the means that lead to the good life for all and for cultivating the necessary moral virtues in the citizenry for achieving that end. The intelligent search for practices conducive to this enterprise that learns from critical reflection on what past experience reveals about what works to increase joy and justice on earth is a recommendation worthy of consideration.[33]

A CRITICAL EVALUATION

Have I succeeded in laying out a clear and distinct alternative to critical realism? I am not sure. I think I may have hinted at a vague and inchoate option! I do retain an element of realism in that reality is one of three points of reference, along with experience and interpretation. My intention is to distinguish my view from critical realism by shifting attention from correspondence to reality to convincing conceptualizations of the experience of reality. We cannot test our theories by comparing them to reality. We have to test them by asking whether they offer coherent schemes elucidatory of the evidence. Do our theories succeed in providing a satisfactory interpretation of experience? The question is not whether our theories are descriptive of reality but whether they are explanatory of experience. Put differently, critical realism assumes a subject-object framework in which the issue turns on the way and extent to which interpretations of the experience by the subject correspond to the reality, i e., the object. Pragmatism abandons or at least deemphasizes this duality in favor of the unity constituted by the indissoluble togetherness of reality (the objective), experience, and interpretation (the subjective).[34]

Does that vanquish or replace realism? No, not totally, since the claim remains that it is reality that is experienced and interpreted but precisely reality *as experienced*. Does this constitute a plausible alternative to critical realism? It seems to me it does. But perhaps I have only succeeded in shifting the emphasis but not creating an alternative to critical realism. Perhaps I should call the result pragmatic realism, i. e., a version of weak critical realism with a heavy stress on pragmatic verification.

What about the relationship of my view to the deconstructionists? I agree with them that history and the contemporary scene exhibit an endless chain of interpretations. That, after all, is one of my main points. Moreover, each interpretation is an interpretation of other interpretations. But is there no referent beyond the text in any sense? If they mean that no interpretation ever connects with reality, that reality is never present in interpretation in any shape, form, or fashion whatsoever, I demur. If they mean merely that reality is never directly or literally or fully present but is present only in interpretation, that the only reality we know is reality as interpreted, then I agree, when allowed to put my own spin on the terms. But if that is what they mean, how do they differ -- in that respect only -- from the critical realists or from my pragmatism?

IS CHRIST THE NORM OF TRUTH?

Some who might be willing at least to entertain the propositions set forth to this point may wish to demur when I draw a further conclusion. I propose that Jesus as represented in Scripture and tradition cannot be the final authority, norm, and judge of beliefs, values, duties, personal virtues, and social policies. For Christians the data available to us in the New Testament and in the history of the interpretive tradition will certainly enter positively and centrally into the determination of all these matters, but what Jesus believed (or what we believe he affirmed) cannot be final or ultimate. What we make of what we take Jesus to have said and done is the work of the interpreter.

Further, I urge that in practice and functionally this is the case anyway, whether or not my own views are accepted or not. It works this way at least in those theologies that construe Jesus in such a way that their favored doctrines are found there. But since the opposing parties attribute contradictory doctrines to Jesus, all cannot be right. Yet each insists on its own truth, since if something is authorized, proposed, or approved by Jesus, it must be true. My thesis is that Jesus as the Christ is a theological device with which we express our own normative beliefs, ideals, and values. Conceptions of Christ typically are mirrors in which we discover our own values. Usually, the suggestion is that Jesus himself held these authorized and authoritative views, and this makes them valid or at least Christianly authentic. This move is necessary to support the underlying proposition, namely, that if Jesus said it, it is true or that Jesus said it because it is true. Either way a congruity must exist between Jesus and truth. I deny that this connection necessarily holds.

Let me illustrate. If Jesus sanctioned slavery or the subordination of women, would that make it authoritative for today? The answer must be no. The usual way to settle this question is for the slaveholders to demonstrate that Jesus did implicitly approve slavery and for the opponents to show that he did not. The same holds for the status of women, traditionalists finding in Jesus an upholder of male supremacy and feminists finding in him an equalitarian with respect to the sexes. But are not slavery and the subordination of women wrong, regardless of what Jesus thought? The stratagem of finding in Jesus our own ideals is not dishonesty, but it is apparent to me that this is exactly what we do. Creativity knows no bounds in conservatives or liberals when it comes to finding in Scripture what fits with their own theologies. Today liberals readily dismiss passages of Scripture that teach disapproved doctrines, whether in the Old Testament or in Timothy. Usually, they hold back from challenging Jesus, preferring to represent him in such a way that he is the author of the views they find compelling and normative. This sometimes means judging particular views of Jesus by his own more basic ideals. On this basis many liberals almost effortlessly reject what Jesus said about the everlasting punishment of the wicked (Matt. 25:41, 46) in favor of universalism or some other alternative nicer than being tossed into the eternal flames.[35] Once we locate that inner core of Gospel truth, we can support or reject whatever we need to, never mind what specific passages say. If a text, however, is favorable, it can be quoted by liberals with a fervor that rivals that of the biblical infallibilists. Fundamentalists have their own ways of letting in and keeping out what does not fit with their larger schemes of belief, including ignoring the offending or troublesome passages. Biblical materials and the infinite possibilities inherent in hermeneutical imagination are such that with skill the stratagem of harmonizing objective norms with subjective proclivities can be successfully carried out by all parties, never mind that they contradict each other right and left.

Was Jesus a feminist or a traditional upholder of male supremacy? Let us employ the best resources and methods available to determine to the extent that we can if Jesus were in fact a feminist, and, if so, in what sense. If we get very precise about what feminism is or must be, the results are likely to be quite uncertain. The logic of my position, however, was stated by Mary Daly, who said that whether Jesus was a feminist or not, she is.[36] The Apostle Paul had good advice:

Finally, . . . whatever is true, whatever is honorable, whatever is just, whatever is pure, whatever is lovely, whatever is gracious, if there is any excellence, if there is anything worthy of praise, think about these things (Phil. 4:8 (RSV).

Certainly what we believe Jesus to have sponsored in the way of beliefs, virtues, obligations, and aspirations enters into the determination of what we take to be true, just, lovely, worthy of praise, and most excellent. Nevertheless, the truth or falsity of something does not depend on whether Jesus affirmed it or not. That judgment must be made in the light of the best we know up to now from all sources, the Jesus of the New Testament being prominent among the clues to what is true, good, and beautiful. My claim is that this is the way it works anyway. We do not allow Jesus functioning as the Christ to have held views that we know (from whatever source) to be either false or immoral. Everyone somehow manages to find in him the normative source and anchor of what is true, moral, and most excellent in all things spiritual, even if some creative exegesis must be employed to accomplish this end.

I think it is better to recognize honestly that operationally we are the final authorities and take responsibility for what we believe. We can acknowledge Jesus to be the source and inspiration of the highest and best that we know, namely, that God loves us and requires us to love one another. Nevertheless, in putting that into a theological and ethical framework for today, we must concede that we are the actual or functional authorities who determine what is normative for belief and practice. It may be useful to do the best we can to discover the person, the words and the deeds of Jesus as a historical figure. We can acknowledge him as the supreme inspiration of our own best ideals and values. But in the end, it is we who are the author of theological doctrines and moral values, even when we assert them to be grounded in a reality not ourselves. All present convictions are subject to criticism, revision, and abandonment, but it is we who must undertake those tasks too as better information or insight demands. At last, when all is said and done, we have no choice but to live by what we judge to be most excellent in the way of belief and practice. This is the case even if our choice is to surrender our autonomy in order to believe and practice what we understand the Bible, Jesus, God, our church, or some other authority to require of us.

NOTES

1. Winston Churchill, House of Commons (May 23, 1940), in *The Sayings of Winston Churchill*, ed. by J. A. Sutcliffe (London: Gerald Duckworth & Co., 1992), 55.
2. See Sallie McFague, *Models of God: Theology for an Ecological, Nuclear Age* (Philadelphia: Fortress Press, 1987).
3. David R. Griffin, *A Process Christology* (Philadelphia: Westminster Press, 1973).
4. Paul Tillich, *Systematic Theology* (Chicago: University of Chicago Press, 1957) II:97-180.
5. In this paragraph I combine two questions: the historical question regarding the extent to which we can have knowledge of the biblical Jesus that corresponds with the reality and the philosophical question regarding what is the case about Ultimate Reality and morality. I am a critically realistic pragmatist on both questions.
6. George Tyrell, *Christianity at the Cross-Roads* (London: Longmans, Green, & Co., 1910), 44.
7. Bruce Barton, *The Man Nobody Knows: A Discovery of the Real Jesus* (Indianapolis: Bobbs-Merrill, 1925). Authors (or publishers) can hardly resist the temptation to provide us with the "real Jesus." Seventy years after Barton, we have Luke Timothy Johnson, *The Real Jesus* (San Francisco: HarperCollins, 1996). But, alas, which "real Jesus" is the "really real" Jesus?
8. Adolf Harnack, *The Essence of Christianity* (New York: Charles Scribner's Sons, 1902); Rudolf Bultmann, *Theology of the New Testament* (New York: Charles Scribner's Sons, 1951), vol. I.
9. James Robinson, *A New Quest of the Historical Jesus* (London: SCM Press, 1959).

10. See *US News and World Report* (April 8, 1996), 46-53, for a popular account of contemporary questers -- Robert Funk, Marcus Borg, John Meier, John Dominic Crossan, and Luke Johnson -- who offer varying portraits of Jesus.

11. Robert W. Funk, with Mahlon H. Smith, *The Gospel of Mark: Red Letter Edition* (Sonoma, CA: Polebridge Press, 1991), is one of many in a series presenting the results of the work of "The Seminar," all published by Polebridge Press.

12. For a good survey of philosophical options in epistemology from Plato to Putnam, see Paul K. Moser and Arnold Vander Nat, eds., *Human Knowledge: Classical and Contemporary Approaches* (New York: Oxford University Press, 1987). So far as I can tell, the main lesson to be learned from this splendid volume is that for every cogent position offered, at least two equally cogent refutations are generated, giving rise to still further attempts to work out the difficulties thought to vitiate previous efforts.

13. For a more extensive exploration of the epistemological maze, see my *Theological Biology: The Case for a New Modernism* (Lewiston: Edwin Mellen Press, 1991), 65-120.

14. Considered in broad terms, as representing realism in some fashion and to some degree are the following: David Tracy, Marjorie Suchocki, Langdon Gilkey, Rosemary Radford Ruether, John Cobb, James Cone, Elisabeth Schüssler Fiorenza, Gordon Kaufman, Sallie McFague, and many others. Reference to the works of these theologians can be found in the endnotes to Chapter II. George Lindbeck is largely an exception to critical realism, but he is a relativist who is willing to leave open the possibility for particular believers to affirm that Christian language corresponds in some sense to reality. For a discussion of these matters and many of these thinkers, see my *Theological Biology*, 1-63.

15. David Tracy proposes that correspondence be interpreted to mean "the consensual truth of warranted beliefs" and that correspondence models of truth be retained as important but not primary. David Tracy, *Plurality and Ambiguity: Hermeneutics, Religion, Hope* (San Francisco: Harper & Row, 1987), 29.

16. For an influential statement of the problem, see Richard Bernstein, *Beyond Objectivism and Relativism: Science, Hermeneutics and Praxis* (Philadelphia: University of Pennsylvania Press, 1985).

17. I wish some of the authors I have read would more often heed the advice I saw on a T-shirt: "Eschew obfuscation." In their writings I frequently have difficulty distinguishing between obscurity and profundity.

18. Compare my description of the absolutist realists and the deconstructionists with that of Sallie McFague. "At this point, the absolutism of fundamentalism and the absolutism of deconstruction are similar: the first insists that only one construction (which is not admitted to be a construction) is true, right, and good, and the second insists that all constructions (which are solely the products of aesthetic playfulness) are equally illusory, with none more true, more right, or better than all the others." *Models of God*, 22. My position on the whole is not far from hers regarding the relation of our theological theories to reality. See, e. g., 21-8, 192n37, 195-6n13.

19. Jacques Derrida: "There is nothing outside the text."

20. Quoted by Adam, *What is Postmodern Biblical Criticism?*, 5.

21. Jean François Lyotard, *The Postmodern Condition* (Minneapolis: University of Minnesota Press, 1984), xxiv. For a discussion of Lyotard and other postmodernists, see Steven Best and Douglas Kellner, *Postmodern Theory: Critical Interrogations* (New York: Guilford Press, 1991).

22. In "The Deconstruction of God," Carl Raschke writes, "Neither language nor human self-awareness conceals any thread of reference to things as they are." *Deconstruction and Theology*, by Thomas J. J. Altizer, et. al. (New York: Crossroad Publishing Co., 1982), 4. In "Body, Text, and Imagination," in the same volume, Charles E. Winquist writes, "What appears in language is not nature but the text. The text is not a mirror but a supplement." Ibid., 43.

23. Some of the theologians focus mainly on the classical symbols of incarnation, crucifixion, and resurrection. "Incarnation *irrevocably* erases the disembodied Logos and inscribes a Word which becomes the script enacted in the infinite play of interpretation." Mark C. Taylor, "Text as Victim," in *Deconstruction and Theology*, 71. Again, he writes, "A death of God (a)theology, which is really a radical Christology, finds its completion in the crucifixion of the individual self and the resurrection of universal humanity. The end (or beginning) is realized through the dissemination of the Word." Ibid., 73. See also the quotation from Thomas J. J. Altizer that follows immediately.

24. "Again, we must underscore our leading thesis: deconstruction is the death of God put into writing." Raschke, ibid., 27. See also the essay by Thomas J. J. Altizer, "History as Apocalypse," ibid, 147-177; and Mark C. Taylor, "Text as Victim," ibid., 58-78.

25. In addition to *Deconstruction and Theology*, the following will provide an entrance into deconstruction in theology: Walter Lowe, *Theology and Difference: The Wound of Reason* (Bloomington: Indiana

University Press, 1993); Mark C. Taylor, *Deconstructing Theology* (New York: Crossroad Publishing Co., 1982); and Mark C. Taylor, *Erring: a Postmodern A/theology* (Chicago: University of Chicago Press, 1984). A helpful introduction to what deconstruction might mean for biblical studies is Adam, *What is Postmodern Biblical Criticism?*, 27-43.

26. There are, of course, other anti-realist points of view in addition to deconstruction. However, for my purposes the question about them would be whether in the total scheme of things proposed by them as Christians whether they believe we are in correspondence, in some sense, with Reality, even though they might make a sharp distinction between personal faith (belief in) and cognitive claims clothed in language and stated in doctrines (belief that).

27. See my *Theological Biology*, 71-4. There I introduce the term "interprience" to indicate that we can only speak of reality in terms of our interpreted experience. Unfortunately, the term has not yet caught on in the wider public.

28. William James, *Pragmatism* (New York: Meridian Books, 1955), 45. James attributed the phrase to Shadworth Hodgson.

29. Is reality, then, some kind of unknown thing-in-itself comparable to the Kantian *ding an sich*, the noumenal realm? Not necessarily. Suppose we define being or the real in the objective sense as having the power to affect another. Reality as object would then be the sum total of all the effects or influences exerted on other existents, following a tradition from Plato to Whitehead. What are realities in themselves? Here I rely again on the Whiteheadian view that in the fundamental sense the world is made up of experiencing entities who are subjects to themselves and objects to each other in a myriad of complex relationships and interactions. Reality, then, is not some unknown background source of experience but is present to experience. Unfortunately, interpretations of experience may be erroneous. I may believe that my cold was caused by getting my wet feet and walking in the cold wind. The correct explanation may be that my cold was caused by a virus. Real effects experienced by the body in this case do not have the objective causes my mind theorizes. All this, of course, is my interpretation of reality based on my experience.

30. Some of us, however, may find joy in intellectual beauty and pursue conceptual elegance beyond what practicality strictly requires. But the experience of that pleasure is itself a kind of practical fruit of rational inquiry and may be enjoyed harmlessly in moderation.

31. Of course, there is always Richard Rorty's "occasional cooperative freshman," who will go along with the view that contrary assertions on important issues are equally worthy.

32. Cf. Jeffrey Stout, *Ethics After Babel: The Languages of Morals and their Discontents* (Boston: Beacon Press, 1988), 82-105.

33. See Richard Rorty, "Pragmatism, Relativism, and Irrationalism," in *Human Knowledge*, 212-21.

34. In the Whiteheadian scheme, of course, all entities are both subjects and objects, depending on whether we view them in terms of what they are in and to themselves and what they are to and for others.

35. See John Hick, *Evil and the God of Love*, rev. ed. (San Francisco: Harper & Row, 1978), 346.

36. Mary Daly, *Beyond God the Father* (Boston: Beacon Press, 1973), 73.

Chapter Seven

H. Richard Niebuhr Revisited and Revised[1]

For me to call for a revision of the thought of H. Richard Niebuhr on a fundamental point of social ethics requires audacity. I was one of his students in the early 1950's and have used *Christ and Culture* as a basic frame of reference for four decades.[1] Over a period of years I have concluded that his thesis needs reframing. Even so, I proceed cautiously, since so much of what I now use to amend his thought, I learned from him.

Niebuhr spoke of Christ **and** culture as two points of reference that Christians make in relating faith and ethics. The assumption is that Christ is to some degree an independent, culture-transcending element that can become one pole of a dialogue. In one sense the problem can, of course, be handily stated in terms of Christ **and**

---

[1] This chapter was published in *Encounter* (Summer, 1996). Used by permission.

culture for working purposes. Many of us have done so with propitious results. Since Christ is in the past and every subsequent generation of believers lives in a moving cultural present, a distinction can be made between them. Christ is available to us in the New Testament and in trajectories of interpretation that constitute the Christian tradition. In deciding how they shall live in the world today Christians can consult those authoritative sources that witness to the person, the words, and the deeds of Jesus, the biblical Christ. Reflection upon the beliefs, values, and practices that prevail in the contemporary social order in which they find their worldly citizenship yields another point of reference -- "culture" -- that can be brought into conversation with "Christ."

My point is that, strictly speaking, this conversation is between part (Christ) and whole (culture) or between Christ and not-Christ within a larger cultural totality that contains both. Christ, though an identifiable component in the dialogue, exists wholly within culture. Culture is the all-inclusive reality that contains a sub-dialogue within itself among those of its members who have a loyalty to Christ. Hence, the dialogue between "Christ" and "culture" is not between two independent factors outside each other or at opposite ends of a polarity. Christ is one element within culture that affects how believers relate to their social environment in so far as it may contain Christian influences, other-than-Christ elements, or what they take to be contrary-to-Christ values. The problem is not one of Christ **and** culture. The only Christ is a Christ **within** some culture, known, believed in, and followed by selves and communities who exhibit various ways of relating themselves to the social and cultural milieu that inescapably affects them. Christians may, of course, see their form of life in relation to the larger society in all the five ways Niebuhr so skillfully outlines. In short, while one can conveniently organize the problem in terms of Christ and culture, it is more accurate to recognize that the culture is the concrete reality in its fullness. Reference to Christ by believers takes place within and is a part of the larger cultural reality.

Notice first of all that all access to Christ is mediated through culture. No direct perception is possible that transcends either the culture in which Jesus appeared or the cultural context of the believer. Many contemporary African Catholic Christians have retained practices of ancestor-worship and polygamy, frowned on by the Vatican. An African bishop, Msgr. Bonifatius Haushiku, commented, "Yes, our Namibian African people have accepted Christ, but this Christ walks too much among us in a European garment."[2] Christ always walks among us in some cultural garment. While we never encounter a culturally unclothed Christ, it might nevertheless be argued that Christ is not identical with the apparel, that we can distinguish between them. In an important but limited sense, I agree, although I shall argue that efforts to make the distinction do not so much reveal a naked Christ as dress him in another outfit looking like the one worn by the interpreters. Furthermore, the reality of Christ and the interpretation of that reality are far more interwoven, organic, indissoluble, and far more difficult to distinguish than are Jesus and his attire.

As already noted, Christ is an identifiable point of reference who can be easily distinguished from all others. He is the Jesus of the New Testament who as, Niebuhr says, cannot be confused with "a Socrates, a Plato or an Aristotle, a Gautama, a Confucius, or a Mohammed, or even with an Amos or Isaiah." The Christ of the New Testament is a particular "person with definite teachings, a definite character, and a definite fate." True, but are we to say that Socrates belongs to culture while Jesus does not? Jesus, too, was of and in culture, albeit a different one from Socrates. Precisely put, then, we speak of the normative character of one cultural person (Jesus) rather than that of another cultural person (Socrates). Moreover, we speak of the authority of this particular cultural person for us who are cultural persons of a different era, not of the authority of someone who was not in and of culture for us who are. This is the main point, all the rest that follows is secondary but important nevertheless.

Niebuhr goes to say that despite all the variety in the interpretations found in post-biblical history, there are "always the original portraits with which all later pictures may be compared and by which all caricatures may be corrected." Furthermore, he acknowledges almost as much relativity in the interpretations of Christ as anyone need contend for. Nevertheless, he maintains that despite the fact that "every description is an interpretation, it can be an interpretation of the objective reality." This is a crucial claim that must be examined closely.

Niebuhr speaks of "an interpretation of the objective reality." My thesis is that, when we get down to specifics, the "interpretation" is more decisive than the "objective reality." The reality exists objectively, let us grant, but it is available to us only in the interpretation. Was Jesus a social reformer? In answering this question, it is not easy to correct caricatures by comparing them with the text of the Gospels. How can we tell the caricatures from the corrections? Today's correction becomes tomorrow's caricature. Whose correction is correct? The "original portraits" are themselves interpretations. Portrait is an apt term here. Moreover, every subsequent interpretation is an interpretation of the original interpretations. Interpretation is a cultural activity that uses culturally-produced methods yielding results stated in culturally-constructed concepts and assessed by culturally-generated criteria. While in the end doubtless some correspondence exists between the original reality and the original and subsequent portraits, every attempt to state exactly *what it is* that corresponds is one more interpretation. There is no uninterpreted real Jesus, by comparison to whom we can tell how well the interpretations correspond to the reality. Finally, functionally, and in fact, it is with somebody's interpretation that we must deal with and act on, regardless of how closely it does or does not match or represent correctly the reality. And we can never be sure how fully it does or does not conform to the original fact that inspired the original portraits. Reality and interpretation are merged so organically that we can never distinguish fully or infallibly which is which. The fundamental point, however, is that both reality and interpretation lie wholly within culture.

Hence, I not so much deny Niebuhr's claim -- that descriptions are interpretations of the reality -- as I question its practical significance. More importantly, the critical question is not who Jesus was or what Jesus said and did but what we believe we are required to so in our situation here and now because of our loyalty to him. Whether Jesus was a social reformer or not, should we be today? It is in answering questions like this that the role of the interpreter is even more decisive.

In the second place, then, let us note that the ways Christians understand the meaning of Christ for today are fundamentally determined by their peculiar cultural inheritance, position in society, life experiences, creative capacities, and idiosyncrasies. Biblical exegesis contributes content and form to the resulting prescription for action. Nevertheless, the Bible can be read by believers as demanding a variety of stances toward the prevailing values and institutions of their social world. Which position groups of Christians adopt is bound up with their location in society and the interests they have and the aims they wish to realize as social beings. That all find in Christ the authority for taking the five stances so well described by Niebuhr is not irrelevant, since the rationale for their contrasting actions can usually be grounded in some plausible reading of the Bible. But what is determinative of the specifics of these varying ways of serving Christ? Is it not primarily contemporary social facts and values rather than past biblical ideals? Christians of all persuasions will rise up in indignant protest to assert that it is Christ they obey not their cultural ethos and among them vehemently offer a full range of contradictory positions as the will of the real Jesus.

All Christians acknowledge that we are required to love our neighbor as we love ourselves. Jesus plainly taught us to do so. It is of immense significance that the obligation is to love the neighbor and not hate or ignore our human companions or destroy them at our whim. Yet this did not prevent Augustine from approving the persecution of heretics, Calvin from consenting to the death of Servetus because of a flaw in his Trinitarianism, James Henley Thornwell from defending slavery on the basis of Scripture and reason, or present-day followers of Jesus from condemning sexual relations between persons of the same sex, even if they live in a faithful monogamous union. The determinative element in each case is a set of beliefs and values that are relative to and culturally contemporaneous with each of the interpreters in question. What of pragmatic import is left of the "objective reality," set forth in these "original portraits," given the fact that other Christians come to contrary and irreconcilable conclusions about love of neighbor in relation to heresy, slavery, and homosexuality? An "objective reality" that is compatible with contradictory ethical injunctions on about every issue you can name in the past and present threatens to dissolve into the various interpretations. The concrete specificity of texts obviously puts some ultimate limits on exegesis, but the extent to which human ingenuity can produce results from Scripture suitable to ones purpose should not be underestimated.

Miracles of hermeneutics can readily find ways to render embarrassing passages harmless or to generate congenial mandates. Note, for example, what liberals do with passages that subordinate women to men, authorize or assume slavery without condemnation, or teach that homosexual practice is an abomination requiring the death sentence to perpetrators. Today not even fundamentalists teach that slavery is biblically approved or that women should not have the right to vote, as eminent theologians -- North and South -- did in the 19th century. The Bible has not changed; cultural consciousness has and, with it, the understanding of what Christ requires in our time.

The contemporary debate in the church over homosexuality is about what the Bible or Christ requires only in an inconsequential sense. How many theological scholars are there who think that the Bible, rightly interpreted and functioning as the Word of God for today, teaches a view of the permissibility of homosexual behavior contrary to their own personal outlook? I do not suggest that integrity is lacking on anyone's part. Neither do I suspect that positions are taken independently of the Bible and then subsequently and deliberately made to conform. The encounter between text and interpreter is more interactive and complex than that. Nevertheless, when the Bible is claimed as the authority for contrary positions regarding homosexuality and many other issues that in each case match the views of the interpreter, we do need to ask what is going on. Usually, each party secretly within its own bosom takes comfort in the certitude that it has correctly heard the Word of God and that those who disagree hold views offensive to Jesus.

In their 1995 meeting in Atlanta the Southern Baptist Convention repented of its racism in the past. This sorrow for sins past occurred long after the cultural consciousness had changed and when it had become safe to be against racial prejudice. Yet my fellow Southern Baptist preachers a generation ago by and large found it easy to accommodate racial segregation to biblical principles. Local Baptist congregations and state conventions were captive to the culture with only a few exceptions to qualify the generalization. Loyalty to Christ notwithstanding, the resistance to racial change among whites from one region of the South to another was pretty much determined by the percentage of blacks in the population rather than by the proportion who professed loyalty to Jesus as personal Savior. It would have been a miracle of gigantic proportions if all -- or even a majority -- of the white Christians in those counties of the South in which blacks were in the majority had upon a fresh contemplation of the Gospels voluntarily opted for democracy and racial equality a half century ago. Yet who would deny that those memorable slogans of the 50's regarding Sunday School growth, flourishing during the civil rights struggle, were expressions of devotion to Christ: "A million more in '54," "Keep'em alive in '55."

During the same period the Civil Rights Movement led by Martin Luther King, Jr. mobilized masses of African American Christians and some whites to challenge the caste system and to transform the culture. This crusade stood in sharp contrast to the culture-accommodating stance of most white churches. Christ was invoked as the inspiration for their conflicting positions by both the protestors and the defenders of the prevailing social order. Was not the moral stance of each party more fundamentally shaped by the social location of the respective groups than by any strictly religious factors? One and the same Christ was appropriated, believed in, and obeyed in radically different ways. Was it not the history and experience of each race that accounted for the difference between white segregationists and black liberationists, since, after all, they were reading the same Bible? King and his followers sought to transform culture, while conservative white preachers exalted a Christ of southern culture. But was it not the culture-determined interpretation not the objective reality of Christ that made the difference? African Americans were in a happy circumstance that united self-interest and biblical justice -- the best of all possible worlds, hermeneutically speaking.

In 1955 when as his pastor I had based my offending racial views on the Bible, a Baptist deacon angrily said to me, "I don't care what the Bible says, we are not going to allow our schools to be integrated." Actually, he did care -- a lot. He was a good man of deep faith and abiding integrity well known for his kindness to persons of both races. All his life he had believed that the Bible permitted segregation, and he still did. He was angry at me for challenging that view. His remark, even if he did later regret making it, indicates how deeply the culture determined his point of view.

It took a denomination in this country that includes Henry VIII in its early days until 1976 to decide that Jesus would consider women fit to administer his body and blood to the faithful. Did that move result initially and primarily from a fresh encounter with Christ, or was it an ecclesiastical parallel to the secular women's movement? And was it the development of a culturally-generated feminist consciousness in some mainly middle-class Christians that led to a search in the Bible for support of equal opportunity for women in the church?

Special difficulties pertain when issues arise that Jesus never faced, e. g., genetic engineering, birth control, race/gender -neutral versus race/gender-preferential policies, fetal-tissue research, health care options (managed competition, a one-payer system, laissez-faire, etc.), assisted suicide, jobs for loggers versus preserving the spotted owl, and on and on. Here the door is open to great divergence of opinion. Conclusions must be reached through a complex network of operating assumptions based eventually on something the interpreter believes to be normative for Christians. By the time specific decisions are reached on these complicated matters, it is not easy to discern anything that is distinctively Christian in contrast to the wisdom offered by secular theorists who occupy the same cultural space. The crucial element is not the Christ in the background but the network of intellectual and moral assumptions that constitutes the interpretive medium through which Christ is made contemporaneous with us. The prohibition against birth control by some ecclesiastical authorities who claim to have a special mandate to interpret the mind of Christ rests on theories about natural law rooted in a specific cultural history. Functionally, "Christ" resolves into the highest and best morality known to the Christian presently speaking, granted that one factor contributing to the ideal being acknowledged is the New Testament portrait of Jesus of Nazareth.

Even on the points to which Jesus spoke directly, the difficulties are not lessened much. Pacifists and just war theorists acknowledge the words and deeds of the same Jesus. The differences between them lie in their human reasoning about the moral legitimacy and pragmatic usefulness of the violent restraint of evildoers, since Jesus and the New Testament can be read either way. Let any new moral crusade arise in contemporary society, and it will appear simultaneously or later in certain segments of the church touted as the mandate of Christ for our time. In what sense is this new turn among believers motivated by authority proceeding directly and immediately from Jesus? Or is it simply a way of adding divine sanction to positions whose more important endorsement is rooted in secular reasoning originated in the culture? Generally speaking, zip codes may be a better indicator of political and social ideology than church membership. Let us grant that influence springing from Christ over the centuries and transmitted through secular and ecclesiastical communities is one element in the culture itself.

Even if some Christians were the first to condemn slavery or to demand justice for women, do not these revolutions occur in the fullness of cultural time among Christians whose peculiar social location opens them to precocious insight? It is not difficult to discern why in 1850 abolitionist sentiment among white Christians flourished in Massachusetts and not in South Carolina. And the difference lies not in the degree of devotion to Christ but in climate, soil, profitability of cotton growing with slave labor, and other thoroughly material and worldly factors. Actually the slaveholders had more specific biblical texts favorable to their position than did the abolitionists, who had to resort to what Nels Ferré called "the larger logic of the Bible."

Nothing I have said about the cultural conformity of the churches would come as new information to H. Richard Niebuhr.

No one was more eloquent than he in exposing the bondage of the followers of Jesus to the provincial ethics of the races, classes, nations, and cultural traditions that define their identity. Everything I have written here about the captivity of Christians to the ethos of their particular time and place is in harmony with the spirit and substance of the first chapter of *The Social Sources of Denominationalism*. I first learned of the social conditioning and historical relativity of the beliefs and practices of the churches from that very book, as well as from *Millhands and Preachers*, written by his colleague Liston Pope. Niebuhr would perhaps only object that I go too far beyond conditioning toward determination.

The social shaping of faith and ethics does not mean that religion is wholly submissive, lacking any initiatory power of its own. In *The Social Sources of Denominationalism*, Niebuhr examined the "influence of social forces on faith," while in *The Kingdom of God in America*, he explored "the faith which is independent, which is aggressive rather than passive, and which molds culture instead of being molded by it." I agree that both sides of the equation must be acknowledged. Religion, a constituent of culture itself, does generate moral energy in persons that has practical consequences. The religious dynamic, however, is best seen in terms of potencies engendered by the Christ-within-culture factor expended to bring Christian behavior into line with the perceived will of God. Transformations of society may result. Marxists have their own problem of Marx and culture. They are empowered by their faith to change the world. Like Christians they connect their earthly vocation to a set of beliefs about ultimate reality and its implications for the outcome of history. Being a Libertarian or belonging to the Hemlock Society may also generate ethical activity that seeks to transform culture on particular points without any necessary accompanying religious dimension or theory of cosmic ultimacy. Nevertheless, all these ways of being a self in the world -- Christian, Marxist, Libertarian, Hemlock Society member -- are intracultural realities. Christ is not an authority transcending all cultures but a point of reference located in a particular past culture believed to be normative for the present.

Niebuhr interpreted the transforming potential of Christianity in terms of "radical monotheism." Faith in God relativises all other values and commitments, convinces us of our sinful devotion to self-interest, and leads to repentance for our idolatry. A genuine encounter of this sort with the Transcendent One may indeed transform our ethical commitments by enlarging our vision and extending our moral concern to all those whom God loves, i. e., the whole of creation and all its creatures. Trust in and loyalty to a Universal Reality who values all beings can have revolutionary implications for how we live in the world. The practice of radical monotheism purges elements of self-interest and partiality cherished in our partisan ways of existing and thinking. It relativises our own perspectives and lead us to acknowledge the validity of the insights and interests of others. This is not a trivial point by any means. It is the primary practical value of radical faith.

However, it is not the specific moral teachings of the New Testament that brings about this revolution but the confrontation with Absolute Transcendence that relativises and judges our present outlook, leading to repentance and a style of life more inclusive of the needs and claims of others. It was not humility, hope, love, or any other moral virtue that filled the soul of Jesus but God, he says. This fits with his claim in *The Meaning of Revelation* that, strictly speaking, revelation bequeaths to us no specific ideas about God and morality. Revelation is the "reconstruction of our natural knowledge about deity," the "conversion and permanent revolution of our human religion through Jesus Christ."[3] Our "natural knowledge" and our "human religion" are cultural products. Meeting the Transcendent Lord converts what we bring to the experience and in this way produces change in behavior and belief. When radical faith is translated into ethics, the specific content and form of behavior is decided contextually by believers using resources available to them in their particular time and place. Only now their commitment is to love the God above all finite gods and goods with their whole being and to love others -- all others -- as God loves them. Radical monotheism has its primary consequence, then, as a judgment against our idolatries, partial perspectives, and limited commitments and as a positive reorienting of life by which believers, to the extent their finite knowledge allows, seek to attune their lives to God's own ends and norms.

I, too, understand the heart of biblical religion this way, partly because of Niebuhr's influence. Unfortunately, pure monotheism as envisioned by Niebuhr is as rare as it is beautiful. For most of us Christians most of the time Christ confirms rather than judges the best we know and do as worshipers of many gods who love ourselves more than we love our neighbors, especially those distant or unlike us. Moreover, radical faith is the ethical equivalent of fidelity to a universal good that includes all instead of allegiance to ends that maximize the partisan interests of some. Hence, Christ understood in terms of radical monotheism is not a non-cultural or supra-cultural factor but the active and compelling imperative implied by the ideal of an all-inclusive community of divinely-valued beings. This norm pronounces judgment on all beliefs, attitudes, and practices that fall short of its demands.

In that remarkable last chapter of his classic work, Niebuhr, as an existentialist and relativist, acknowledges that no resolution of the problem of Christ and culture can be found in the realm of theoretical thought. It is not possible to say of any perspective that this is **the** Christian answer. Intellectual inquiry yields only relativities and partial perspectives, none of which is fitting for all people for all times and places. The only settlement comes through decision in some present moment by selves and communities using their best insights. Commitments, however, though always relative are ideally made in faith. Faith is loyalty to and trust in the One Absolute Power and Goodness who knits the limited knowledge, fragmentary perspectives, and circumscribed deeds of all particular selves and communities into a universal pattern beyond our ken that ultimately transforms the cultures of this world into the Divine Community.

My alternative belief in a Finite, Suffering Struggling God living in and through the adventure of cosmic and cultural history does not permit me to share his neo-Calvinist convictions about divine sovereignty. This theological difference leads me to reverse the last sentence of the book. Niebuhr writes that we make our decisions "in view of the fact that the world of culture -- man's achievement -- exists within the world of grace -- God's Kingdom." My view is that the world of grace exists within the world of culture. Niebuhr upholds a universal outlook in one way; I aspire toward an all-embracing inclusiveness in another. Both of us abandon the Augustinian notion that history is the tale of two cities. Only one city -- the community that includes all living beings -- is the locus of God's redemptive activity. The world in all its fullness, with all its heart-breaking tragedy and massive suffering along with its fragile joys and frequent pleasures, is the arena of Divine Creativity. The church exists within that larger realm and is one community among many in which the aims of God may be furthered or hindered. Human civilization itself is a part of the larger realm of earthly and cosmic history within which Divine Creativity works to actualize the potentials for enjoyment constantly arising in living beings. God is the Life of the world, which is the Body of God. It is in culture that God works to bring the human community to the highest level of justice and happiness possible.

I agree that Christians must resolve the question of their loyalty to Christ by decisions made in the absence of objective certainty. As an existentialist and voluntarist, Niebuhr views commitment as a leap from thought to action. Decision is a different order of activity from theoretical thinking, but it involves theoretical thinking nevertheless.[4] He is a kind of pragmatist in that the reasoning of faith is of the heart and not the head. It is the practical thinking of an involved self in search of personal meaning not of a disinterested observer in quest of theoretical truth. As a different sort of pragmatist, I would urge that choice is the expression of our best thinking in the attempt to create and relate means and ends in the never ending quest for practical solutions that maximize total satisfaction as determined by testing options experientially. One element that must be satisfied is the demand that theory unite logical coherence with experiential adequacy in accounting for relevant data. No claim is made that the preferred theory corresponds to reality but only that it makes more sense to the interpreter than available alternatives and works well in practice when tested experientially. Objective uncertainty reigns. We can only claim that our actions in quest of the good and in obedience to the right are more satisfactory theoretically and practically than any so far discovered options. Decisions, though fully rational in this pragmatic sense, never lose their relativity but many of them, though not all, may nevertheless contribute beneficially to the World Adventure that is God's own Life. History has a tragic character, so that some evil is never fully redeemed.

What is the conclusion of the matter? The important consideration is not that my naturalistic theism posits an immanent God in contrast to his Neo-Reformation doctrine of divine sovereignty. Nor is it that I overlearned my lesson from him about historical relativity and hence risk dissolving all objective realities into subjective interpretations. The main point is that the problem of "Christ" and "culture" has to do with the relationship of two intracultural elements, not something non-cultural in relation to culture. Jesus of Nazareth emerged in a particular time and place and culture. He is the Christ to whom Christians want to be loyal in their own time and place and culture. Both Lord and follower are in and of culture, totally. Disciples look not to a Christ who is outside, beyond, or transcendent to culture but to a real person whose existence is completely within and a part of some past culture but believed to offer enduring wisdom, grace, and hope for all cultures. Their task is to discern the meaning of that past cultural event for present cultural events. In that sense, Christians do engage in a dialogue with Christ **and** culture to discover the implications of the former for the latter. The conversation with Christ, however, is not with some non-cultural reality but with a person who speaks from within one culture to persons within another who find in him a compelling source of truth about God and life. The problem of Christ and culture has to do with the relationship between two cultural realities -- the Christ of that past culture and the specific culture of some subsequent generation of believers.

The proposed restatement is, of course, accomplished by definitional magic, so that anything done on this earth by human beings, especially in terms of the creation of enduring beliefs, values, and symbols, is included within culture. While the Christ of the Bible is the focal point of discussion among Christians and the norm by which they aspire to judge all institutions and practices, all takes place within and is a part of culture. It might be argued that Christians believe that Jesus the man was also God or at least spoke with the authority of God and therefore, in that sense, was and is transcultural. Even so, once having entered history in the person, language, and deeds of Jesus, the Word of God, wholly and totally, became part of the world of culture, at least in so far as that Word is expressed in form and content intelligible to human beings.

NOTES

1. H. Richard Niebuhr, *Christ and Culture* (New York: Harper & Row, 1951).
2. *New York Times*, May 1, 1994, 16.
3. I have never been sure how far Niebuhr takes this point. Is revelation in the strictest sense purely an existential event wholly void of or disconnected from intellectual content in which all our loyalties are relativised and refocused through a single-minded loyalty to God, so that all things are subsequently valued in their relation to God's valuing of them rather than having some independent value that compromises radical faith? Is it a totally internal, personal awareness of our divided worship, our devotion to many gods, that judges us, incites repentance, and leads toward trusting the God above all gods and a reordering of commitments in the direction of universalizing and intensifying our commitments? Or is the intellectual content there but just not the important thing? And does it matter which ideas, doctrines, beliefs constitute our natural religion? Can the doctrinal content of our natural religion be judged by definable criteria? Must beliefs to be valid be in conformity with the Bible and its teachings about God, creation and its goodness, love, the promise of future redemption, and so on? Or could the radicalizing stance be abstracted from biblical doctrines and Israel's history and applied to the Socratic virtues or Buddhist practice?
4. Complex issues arise here, and it appears to me that Niebuhr was not always as clear as he might have been. The distinction between thinking and deciding, on the one hand, and between theoretical and practical thinking, on the other hand, seem to me to get conflated at times (e. g., *Christ and Culture*, 241, bottom). Even when thinking as an involved self in quest of personal meaning, one needs to undertake dispassionate

theoretical inquiry regarding what is real and valuable. Moreover, when one has come to a conclusion theoretically about what is real and valuable while thinking existentially as a self in search of salvation, one still has to decide practically, i. e., act upon one's conclusions. If the important thing is not to determine what Christianity is but to become a Christian (Kierkegaard), one still has to have a theory about Christianity in the process of becoming a Christian in practice. In reading *The Meaning of Revelation*, I often got confused trying to figure our when and how "internal history" was different from "external history" and when the former required or even became identical with the inquiries, procedures, and norms of the latter. It seems to me that "internal history" requires "external history" as part of its functioning, while "external history" can involve purely speculative, disinterested inquiries without ever being compromised by existential concern or decisions affecting ones existence. Existential concern, however, always requires disinterested inquiry as preparation for or in connection with making personal commitments. However, thinking of whatever sort never is equivalent to deciding or acting, which is a different kind of operation. Maybe this is what Niebuhr himself believed. Either I am confused about this, or Niebuhr made it more complicated than it need be or both.

Chapter Eight

The Ethics of Capital Punishment

What are the implications of a new modernism as conceived in these pages for ethics? The approach outlined here is deeply critical of traditional views of the Bible, God, and Christ. The claim throughout has been that contemporary believers must judge all doctrines relating to faith and practice by the best they know from all sources up to now, the Bible and Christian tradition being foremost among them. I have argued that while this way of doing theology poses serious questions for Christian unity and identity, compelling reasons dictate that this risk be taken for the sake of more important gains. Christian identity is in such dispute anyway in theory and pretty well shattered in practice, so that a few modernists added to the mix will not further damage the unity of the tradition. A more important consequence of modernism has to do with the ethical principles and practices that flow from its method and its peculiar doctrines. Ethics in theory and in practice is a fruit of theology and faith, and Jesus urged that it was by our fruits that our deepest identity is constituted. The purpose of this chapter is to illustrate how one contemporary modernist approaches an issue much in debate at the present time.

NORMS OF CHRISTIAN ETHICAL PRACTICE

In previous works I have written on Christian ethics in relation to a variety of individual and social issues.[1] My approach was in terms of the normative principles of Christian thought as they lead to specific behaviors and policies under given circumstances. Contextually, my outlook was developed in debate with Reinhold Niebuhr.[2] The highest form of rational ethics according to Niebuhr is *mutual love* -- a giving and receiving in which all parties are considered equal in value. While there is much to commend this ideal, he believes that it is unstable and will tend to degenerate into a calculation of benefits and ultimately disintegrate. Each party will ask whether as much love is being returned as is being offered. Niebuhr is correct, I think, if one assumes that mutual love is conditional upon an equality of contribution and reward. *Conditional mutual love* says, "I will love you as much as you love me but only as long as I am getting as much as I give."

Niebuhr argues that *mutual love* must be constantly replenished by *sacrificial love* that is rooted in a faith in a transcendent God and thus not bound to this world's goods and standards only. Niebuhr thinks that *sacrificial love* is the core meaning of *agape* in the New Testament. *Agape* so understood stands as a transcendent standard beyond all human achievement, an "impossible possibility" that is yet relevant to every moral situation as judge, guide, and inspiration. This form of love is modeled after the example of Jesus on the cross. It sacrifices self in order to serve the other. It risks all and gives all, heedless of the self's own needs, wants, and interests. This love goes the second mile, resists not one who is evil, gives to every one who would borrow, returns good for evil, and so on (Mt. 5:38-48). I find this unqualified imperative to be morally inadequate in that it neglects necessary discriminations among persons and circumstances, puts no limits on obligation, and has no place for merit. It indiscriminately and indeterminately requires the weak to sacrifice for the strong, the sick to sacrifice for the healthy, the poor to sacrifice for the rich, the virtuous to sacrifice for scoundrels, and the oppressed to sacrifice for the oppressor. Without some guard against this implication, justice is violated, and the worth, integrity, and dignity of the self are compromised.

This way of putting it may be unfair to Niebuhr in not sufficiently representing his full outlook. First of all, he does include mutuality, reciprocity, and equality as valid considerations. Sometimes reciprocity does obtain, and in this fact is to be found the moral component in history. Sometimes love is not returned, and in this is to be found the tragic dimension of life. Secondly, since we are all sinners who constantly fall short of the ideal of *agape*, the main value of this "impossible possibility" in Niebuhr's thought is that it (1) judges us and brings us to repentance and (2) indicates the direction a transformation of life should take. He creates a paradox by combining (a) the recognition that since we fail so miserably to serve our neighbor's good, we are utterly dependent on grace and forgiveness (justification) with (b) a positive hope for progress toward a more holy life and the achievement of justice (sanctification). He holds these two dimensions in dialectical tension so that each corrects the other in a dynamic process with no fixed or final resolution. Hence, given his emphasis on the persistence of sin in the life of the redeemed, the extreme consequences of living a wholly sacrificial life seldom arise except in the rare saint. *Agape* is primarily a judgment on the non-sacrificial life we ordinarily lead not an ideal likely to be wholeheartedly practiced enough that it threatens to demean the personhood of those who live heedless of their own needs and just claims. Saints may understand self-sacrifice as a vocational hazard voluntarily assumed and thus an expression of their authentic selfhood rather than as a violation of it. Moreover, Jesus himself could exemplify the fullness of sacrificial love only by becoming powerless on the cross, lifted above the complexities, ambiguities, and unavoidable compromises of actual life on this earth. This is a powerful moral perspective.

Nevertheless, I contend against Niebuhr that *agape* is not fundamentally sacrificial in which the self is totally heedless of its own needs and interests as it seeks to serve the neighbor.[3] Rather, *agape* should be thought of as *mutual love* that regards the self and the neighbor as equals in a community of equals, with equal rights, opportunities, responsibilities, and privileges. One who practices *agape* will sacrifice for the neighbor when the neighbor's need exceeds one's own or when the larger good of the community requires it but likewise will resist appropriately any trespass against the legitimate needs, claims, and interests of the self. Later, I will refine this analysis by distinguishing between the ethical and the ecstatic dimensions of love.

I propose that *agape* should be defined as *unconditional mutual love*. It does not depend on the response of the neighbor (Mt. 5: 43-48). It continues to seek equality, mutuality, and reciprocity, even when the other reacts with hostility or indifference or in a self-seeking way. *Unconditional mutual love* says, "I will love you on and on no matter what you do, regarding your needs equal to mine and my needs equal to yours." *Unconditional mutual love* includes an element of justice for the self as well as for others and insists that all count for one and no more than one when goods are to be distributed. The moral ideal is that each person shall have the best life possible within the constraints posed by mutual self-realization. The just and good society will seek to maximize the freedom, well-being, and equality of all citizens consistent with the appropriate limits each imposes on the others.

Agape seeks a community in which all persons are regarded as equal in worth and deserving of equal consideration. It seeks a union of persons in a mutually beneficial, reciprocal relationship among free and equal members. However, inequalities of reward and responsibility may arise contextually, since people differ in ability, merit, and need. Excepting only those based on merit and natural ability, inequalities of power, wealth, and authority are legitimate only as pragmatic adjustments necessary to serve the larger and overriding ideal of a community of free and equal persons ruled by the quest of the best life possible for all. Some inequalities, then, are unavoidable, some are necessary, and some are justifiable.[4] It is hard to improve on the principle that requires from each according to ability and gives to each according to need, while not ignoring merit. Justice and love are apposites that mutually require, limit, and complete each other.

The procedure is not to begin with abstract principles and then to apply them but to start with a given situation as it has developed historically and ask in the light of the ideals of a just and good society what steps would improve society. Working out the requirements of justice in the context of the complexities, tragedies, contradictions, contingencies, and ambiguities of real life will tax the best of minds and make for much conflict among even people of good will, exacerbated by the abounding tendencies toward egocentrism and selfishness, not to mention ignorance, foolishness, and shortsightedness. For society as a whole the best that can be hoped for is a temporary, workable rough approximation of the norm with many imperfections. I agree with Niebuhr, however, that history presents indeterminate possibilities of good and that no prior limits should be placed on the extent to which justice and the good life may be achieved. The ideal is, as he says, both transcendent to every actual state of affairs and relevant to every situation as judge, guide, and inspiration. As Alfred North Whitehead said, the ethical absolutes of the early Christians were impractical for governing the Roman Empire, but for that very reason these unattainable ideals served as a gauge of the defects of society and thus "spread the infection of an uneasy spirit."[5] The remainder of the chapter seeks to illustrate this type of ethical thinking by outlining a position on the death penalty.

THE ETHICS OF CAPITAL PUNISHMENT

I was sitting at my computer in my study in Rochester, New York, when the noon news summary came on the radio. Gov. George Pataki had just signed a bill making New York the 38th state to enact a death penalty. For years only the veto power of Democratic governors had prevented this outcome. A majority of the people had long wanted what Gov. Pataki now gave them. When I heard the announcement, I was writing a speech for a local church group offering a theological perspective on the death penalty setting forth two theses:

Thesis one: abstractly and in principle, a case can be made on moral grounds both supporting and opposing capital punishment.

Thesis two: concretely and in practice, compelling arguments against capital punishment can be made on the basis of its actual administration in our society.

Two different cases can be made. One is based on justice and the nature of a moral community. This leads to a reasonable defense of capital punishment. The second is based on love and the nature of an ideal spiritual community. This leads to a rejection of capital punishment.

JUSTICE AND NATURE OF MORAL COMMUNITY

A central principle of a just society is that every person has an equal right to "life, liberty, and the pursuit of happiness." Within that framework, an argument for capital punishment can be formulated along the following lines: some acts are so vile and so destructive of community that they invalidate the right of the perpetrator to membership and even to life. A community founded on moral principles has certain requirements. The right to belong to a community is not unconditional. The privilege of living and pursuing the good life in society is not absolute. It may be negated by behavior that undermines the nature of a moral community. The essential basis on which community is built requires each citizen to honor the rightful claims of others. The utter and deliberate denial of life and opportunity to others forfeits ones own claim to continued membership in the community, whose standards have been so flagrantly violated. The preservation of moral community demands that the shattering of the foundation of its existence must be taken with utmost seriousness. The preciousness of life in a moral community must be so highly honored that those who do not honor the life of others make null and void their own right to live.

Justice requires that punishment fit the crime. Those who deliberately, wrongfully, and in cruelty with malice aforethought violate the personhood of others, especially if this is done persistently as a habit must pay the ultimate penalty. This punishment must be inflicted for the sake of maintaining the community whose foundation has been violated. We can debate whether some nonlethal alternative is a fitting substitute for the death penalty. A life sentence with no possibility of parole is the usual proposal made, and it has much to commend it. But the standard of judgment is whether the punishment fits the crime and sufficiently honors the nature of moral community.

LOVE AND AN IDEAL SPIRITUAL COMMUNITY

Agape, Christian love, is unconditional. It does not depend on the worthiness or merit of those to whom it is directed. It is persistent in seeking the good of others regardless of whether they return the favor or even deserve to be treated well on the basis of their own incessant wrongdoing. An ideal community would be made up of free and equal citizens devoted to a balance between individual self-fulfillment and the advancement of the common good. Communal life would be based on mutual love in which equality of giving and receiving was the norm of social practice. Everyone would contribute to the best of ability, and each would receive in accordance with legitimate claims to available resources.

What would a community based on this kind of love do with those who committed brutal acts of terror, violence, and murder? Put negatively, it would not live by the philosophy of "an eye for an eye, a tooth for a tooth, and a life for a life." It would act to safeguard the members of the community from further destruction. Those who had shown no respect for life would be restrained, permanently if necessary, so that they could not further endanger other members of the community. But the purpose of confinement would not be vengeance or punishment. Rather an ideal community would show mercy even to those who had shown no mercy. It would return good for evil. The aim of isolation is reconciliation and reclamation. Wrongdoers are offered forgiveness. Love never gives up. It is ever hopeful that even the worse among us can be redeemed so that their own potential contribution to others can be realized. Opportunities for confronting those who had been hurt most could be provided to encourage remorse and reconciliation. If a life has been taken, no full restitution can be made, of course, but some kind of service to the community might be required as a way of partially making amends.

EVALUATION

Such in brief is the argument for and against capital punishment, one founded on justice and the nature of moral community, the other resting on love and the nature of an ideal spiritual community. If we stand back from this description and make an attempt at evaluation, one point is crucial. The love ethic requires a high degree of moral achievement and maturity. It is more suitable for small, closely-knit communities in which members know each other personally and in some depth. Forgiveness and reclamation flourish best in a setting in which people can participate in each other's lives. If you press the *agape* motif to its highest manifestation, it becomes an ethic of non-resistance to evil, unqualified pacifism, and self-sacrifice in which self-interest is totally abandoned. The non-resisting Jesus on the cross who surrenders his life to save others is the epitome of *agape* at this level.

Love at this point becomes superethical. It is grounded in a deep faith in God that surrenders any reference to earthly justice. That is the reason for speaking of love and the nature of an ideal **spiritual** community. Love of this kind abandons the right to kill another in self-defense and will refuse absolutely to kill enemies even in a just war. If made into a social ethic, it requires the poor to sacrifice for the rich, the sick to sacrifice for the healthy, the oppressed to sacrifice for the oppressor. It is going the second mile, lending to everyone who would borrow without regard for ability to repay, and not resisting one who is evil. It allows the neighbor to be terrorized, brutalized, and slaughtered, since restraint of the aggressor is forbidden. All this is indefensible on moral grounds.

To make sense of this, it is helpful to distinguish between an ethical dimension of love and an ecstatic dimension. Love as an ethical ideal seeks a community based on mutuality and reciprocity in which there is an equality of giving and receiving. Mutual love has a justice element in which every person has an equal claim to fulfillment and an equal duty to be responsible. Ethical love is unconditional and will reach out to others even when they lack merit. But it will resist encroachment upon its own equal claim to fulfillment and will repel if possible any denial of ones own right to be fully human in every respect. Against the pacifist, ethical love would justify killing in self-defense and killing enemies in a just war when non-lethal alternatives are unavailable. They are necessary and tragic emergency means here and now to stop present and ongoing violence. Capital punishment is opposed since the crime has already been committed, and isolation can protect society against future violence.

Love in the ecstatic dimension becomes superethical. In ecstasy one is delirious with impetuous joy in the presence of the other and totally devoted to that person's happiness and well-being. In ecstasy we do not count the cost to ourselves but are totally self-giving, heedless of our own needs. In this mood sacrifice for the other is not an ethical act of self-denial but the superethical expression of what we most want to do. Ecstasy involves the unpremeditated overflow of boundless affection and the impulsive joy of exhilarating union with the loved one. The ecstatic lover dances with delight in the presence of the beloved. Sensible calculations balancing rights and duties have no place. Rational ethics has been transcended by spiritual ecstasy. Ecstatic love is not an ethical norm. It is a description of how we will act spontaneously in a certain frame of spirit. Love expressed in ecstasy gives all without regard to whether the recipient has any claim on the gift. It is pure grace.

Consider the story of the woman who poured expensive perfume on the head of Jesus (Mk. 14: 3-9)? She was displaying love in the ecstatic dimension. Some present were thinking ethically. They complained that this perfume could have been sold and the proceeds given to the poor. On ethical grounds they were right. What the woman did was indefensible as a moral act. It was irrational and superethical. This deed flowed spontaneously from ecstatic love.

Ecstatic love, however, flows at one point into the rational ethical realm. Here it becomes a felt obligation to be self-sacrificial when the larger good of the community requires it or when the neighbor's need is greater than one's own. As I wrote previously:

> The example of Jesus on the cross can be seen as the overflowing of love so great, so rich, so full, so pure that it willingly sacrifices all, even life, itself, for the sake of the beloved. Or it can be seen as a vocational necessity required of Jesus because no lesser means than the sacrifice of life could have been the instrument of salvation for the community. The nature of *agape* is expressed in either interpretation.[6]

Love has both an ethical and an ecstatic or superethical dimension, and we should not confuse the two. It is quite clear, however, that neither ecstatic nor self-sacrificial ethical *agape* can be the norm of large, impersonal societies. A corporation cannot exist on the basis of forgiving seventy times seven an incompetent employee whose repeated ineptness is costing thousands of dollars. A bank cannot lend money without regard to the ability of the borrower to repay. Ecstasy is not even the mode in which we can live all the time in the most exemplary family life with spouses and children. Ecstatic love is an occasional, fabulous, wonderful overflowing of spectacular affection that adds immeasurably to the joy of life, but it cannot be the day to day standard for ordinary life even in the family or the church.

Can Christian love in the ethical sense be an appropriate norm for a large, secular, pluralistic, civil society? Can unconditional love for the other that regards the welfare of the neighbor equal with ones own be the ideal expected of the citizens of New York or the United States? Can Americans be expected to sacrifice their own self-interests for their more needy neighbors? Surely, to agree with Reinhold Niebuhr, that would be to hope for an "impossible possibility." Ethical love is a description of ideal life in one-to-one encounters, the family, the church, and other small communities in which unconditional regard for each other can be lived out in face-to-face relationships. Even in these settings, we will often fail, but we can hold it up as the criterion by which we are judged and to which we aspire even in our shortcoming. In this sense, ethical love is the supreme norm that serves as both goal and judge of all achievement in every sphere of life and at every level of society. Realistically, however, we can hope only for some rough approximation with decreasing levels of attainment as we move away from intimate communities toward larger collectives. Nation states are not likely, even occasionally, to become ecstatic or self-sacrificing in their devotion to each other! Mutual, not even to mention sacrificial, love is hardly the guiding rule of relations between General Motors and Toyota, nor does either have aspirations in that direction. We should not expect them to.

A workable ethical standard for the state and the nation will appeal to the ideals defined by the requirements of a moral community. To say it otherwise, ethical love expressed as social policy for large, impersonal societies takes the form of justice. What that norm involves for New York or the United States as secular, pluralistic societies cannot be spelled out here.[7] Within this framework a debatable case can be made for capital punishment. Pragmatically and politically, of course, Christians have to work within the framework of justice as defined by the secular society in which they have their citizenship and seek to transform it in the light of their own ideals.

PRACTICAL CONSIDERATIONS

This brings me to thesis two. **The most compelling arguments against capital punishment can be made on the basis of its actual administration in our society.** I will list five of the usual points.

1. **The possibility of error.** Sometimes a person might be put to death who is innocent.
2. **Unfair administration.** Capital punishment is inflicted disproportionately on the poor and minorities.
3. **Weakness of the argument from deterrence.** The claim that the threat of capital punishes reduces violent crime is inconclusive, certainly not proven, extremely difficult to disprove, and morally suspect if any case.

4. **The length of stay on death row.** If there were ever any validity to the deterrence argument, it is negated by the endless appeals, delays, technicalities, and retrials that keep persons condemned to death waiting for execution for years on end. One of the strongest arguments right now against capital punishment is that we are too incompetent to carry it out. That incompetence becomes another injustice.

5. **Mitigating circumstances.** Persons who commit vicious crimes often have a life history filled with poverty, unemployment, abuse, neglect, emotional trauma, violence, cruelty, abandonment, lack of love, and a host of destructive social conditions. These extenuating circumstances may have damaged their humanity to the point that it is unfair to hold them fully accountable for their wrongdoing. Corporate responsibility somehow has to be factored in to some degree. No greater challenge to social wisdom exists than this.

The conclusion of the matter is that capital punishment as presently practiced is a moral disgrace. The irony is that the very societies that have the least right to inflict it are precisely the ones most likely to do so. The compounding irony is that the economic malfunctions and cultural diseases in those same societies contribute to the violence that makes it necessary to unleash even more repression and brutality against its unruly citizens to preserve order and stave off chaos. The fact that our prisons are so full is the most eloquent testimony imaginable of our dismal failure to create a good society. Massive incarceration indicates the bankruptcy of social wisdom and social will. It points to the shallowness of our dedication to solving the basic problems of poverty, moral decay, racial prejudice, class snobbery, meaninglessness, and social discord. Meanwhile, our leaders divert our attention with the alluring fantasy that capital punishment will make our citizens more secure against violent crime.

THE CHURCH AND CHRISTIAN WITNESS

What, then, is the role of the church? It is two-fold. (1) Ideally and ultimately, followers of Jesus are the salt of the earth, light of the world, leaven in the secular loaf. As such, Christians go into the world with the aim of moving, lifting, and luring society in the direction of ethical love. The vocation of Christians is to hold up ethical love as a transcendent gauge exhibiting the moral defects of society and thus "spread the infection of an uneasy spirit."[8] This work will involve both political action and cultural transformation.

(2) Pragmatically and immediately, Christians will translate ethical love into mandates of social justice and work for the best that is possible within given circumstances. Hence, Christian witness may be but is not necessarily directed against capital punishment on moral grounds in principle. The choice is a matter of pragmatic discernment in the situation. In any case, the testimony of the church for the present in this country should be twofold. **A.** Christians should insist that if capital punishment is to be practiced, it must be administered in a just way. On this count, present-day society fails miserably. **B.** Christians should work to overcome the larger injustices, social disarray, and cultural illnesses that create an atmosphere conducive to violence.

To the degree that society provides opportunities for all citizens to achieve a good life in a sensible culture, it is reasonable to believe that the sort of crimes that create the demand for capital punishment will be reduced. The Christian witness to society is this: The present practice of capital punishment is morally abhorrent. If the death penalty is to be employed, first show that it can be administered justly and efficiently, and then we will debate with you whether capital punishment is in principle necessary, fitting, and right or whether a humane society will find non-lethal alternatives that protect citizens from persistently violent criminals. Until then the church should say "no" to this extreme measure.

In all of this I speak of the normative or ideal role of the church related to capital punishment, as I see it. As I have noted many times in previous chapters, the ethical views on this and other issues found in churches and their membership represent the Christian tradition as mediated through their own particular history, cultural background, and social location. Hence, their outlook may be more shaped by such worldly factors as race, region, nationality, class, and the like than by anything that can be identified as Christian as such, although the Bible may be acknowledged as the source and norm of their beliefs and practices. Of course, what holds for other Christians also holds for me. To be candid about this and to admit that I offer my own interpretation rather than some universally valid perspective that can be called *the real Christian view* is part of what it means to be a new modernist. If among them Christians present a variety of contradictory views on personal and social ethical matters, what is the point of any or all of them maintaining, Bible in hand, that they have the one and only authentic message authorized by Jesus himself and representing an absolutely objectively true account of things?

The news summary went off, and the classical music came back on. I pondered for a moment the announcement that New York now has a death penalty law on the books. Presumably, I should feel safer now, but I didn't, really. I returned to the computer screen and continued to work on my speech.

Notes

1. See my *Christian Biopolitics* (Nashville: Abingdon Press, 1971); *Process Ethics* (Lewiston: Edwin Mellen Press, 1984); and *The Passion for Equality* (Totowa, NJ: Rowman & Littlefield, 1987).

2. See his *An Interpretation of Christian Ethics* (New York: Harper & Brothers, 1935); *The Nature and Destiny of Man*, One vol. ed. (New York: Charles Scribner's Sons, 1949), II:68-97, 244-86; and *Faith and History* (New York: Charles Scribner's Sons, 1949), 171-95.

3. For a more detailed discussion of the ethical thought of Niebuhr along with a statement of my own position, see my *Process Ethics*, 125-94.

4. See *The Passion for Equality*, 2-30.

5. Alfred North Whitehead, *Adventures of Ideas* (New York: Mentor Books, 1955), 25.

6. *Process Ethics*, 163.
7. A more extensive discussion of my views on justice and the good society can be found in *Process Ethics*, 195-310, and in *The Passion for Equality*, 63-98.
8. Whitehead, *Adventures of Ideas* , 25.

Index of Names

Allen, Woody, 6
Alexander, Samuel, 102n10
Angley, Ernest, 57
Aronowitz, Stanley, 107n35
Augustine, 3, 47, 51, 139
Ayer, A. J., 6

Barclay, William, 35
Barth, Karl, 7, 104n29
Barton, Bruce, 114
Bultmann, Rudolf, 3, 53, 114

Cage, John, 61-62
Calvin, John, 3, 11, 16, 46, 50-51, 54, 139, 153
Case, Shirley Jackson, 20
Cobb, John B., Jr., 7-8, 18, 65, 130n14
Collingwood, R. G., 101n10
Cone, James, 9-11, 18, 26n 20, 64, 65, 72, 130n14

Daly, Mary, 11, 12, 13, 127
Darwin, Charles, 63
Davaney, Sheila Greeve, 13-14
DeFazio, William, 107n35
Derrida, Jacques, 6, 119, 131n19
Dewey, John, 6

Ferré, Nels, 55
Fosdick, Harry Emerson, 62, 65
Frei, Hans, 6
Freud, Sigmund, 20
Funk, Robert W., 115

Gadamer, Hans-Georg, 49
Gilkey, Langdon, 16, 17, 105n29, 130n14
Graham, Billy, 72
Griffin, David R., 111

Hardesty, Nancy, 26
Harnack, Adolf, 11, 12, 53, 114
Hartshorne, Charles, vii, 101
Hawking, Stephen W., 100n1, 100n2
Heidegger, Martin, 6
Hegel, Georg F. W., 63
Hick, John, 51, 60n5

James, William 122, 123
Jones, William R., 18

Kaufman, Gordon, 29n45, 65, 103n22, 130
Kierkegaard, Soren, 20, 150n4
King, Martin Luther, Jr., 57, 96, 141

167

Kolakowski, Leszek, 31
Lindbeck, George, 6, 23, 58, 65, 130n14
Loomer, Bernard, vii, 28n31, 74, 81, 102
Luther, Martin, 3, 11, 72, 153
Lyotard, Jean François, 119
Marx, Karl, 20, 63, 144
Mathews, Shailer, 2, 20, 21, 22, 24n1, 29, 32, 58, 63, 65. 81
McFague, Sallie, 65, 109, 1130n14, 130n18, 131
McNeill, John, 37
Meland, Bernard, vii
Mollenkott, Virginia, 38
Moltmann, Jurgen, 4, 17, 18, 28n40, 105

Niebuhr, H. Richard, x, 135-150
Niebuhr, Reinhold, 3, 16, 19, 64, 65, 95, 152-3, 155, 160
Nietzsche, Friedrich, 6, 20
Nozick, Robert, 61

Pannenberg, Wolfhart, 17, 104n29, 105
Pataki, George, 155
Pittenger, Norman, 38
Plato, 101, 102, 132n29
Pope, Liston, 144

Raschke, Carl, 131n22, 131n24
Rauschenbusch, Walter, 11, 64, 65
Roberts, Oral, 56
Rorty, Richard, 6, 132n31
Ruether, Rosemary Radford, 11, 13, 27n29, 64, 65, 130n14

Russell, Bertrand, 6
Russell, Letty, 27n27

Sartre, Jean Paul, 6
Scanzoni, Letha, 26n22, 38
Schüssler Fiorenza, Elisabeth, 12, 13, 23, 27n29, 65, 72 130n14
Stout, Jeffrey, 73
Suchocki, Marjorie Hewitt, 130n14
Taylor, Mark C., 131n23
Thornwell, James Henley, 139
Tillich, Paul, 3, 29n49, 52, 65, 95, 111
Tracy, David, 4-7, 25n10, 25n11, 25n13, 130n14
Tribble, Phyllis, 27n27

West, Cornell, 119
Whitehead, Alfred North, vii, 6, 17, 29n44, 63, 100n6, 101, 102n10, 102n16, 104, 132n29, 133n34, 155, 163
Wieman, Henry Nelson, vii, 20, 65, 102
Winquist, Charles E., 131n22

Index of Topics

African American theology,
 4, 8, 9-11
agape, 40, 152-64
 See also, love
agnosticism, 78
authority, the question of, ix-x,
 4-15, 31-42, 45-75

Bible, the, vii-viii, 4-15, 31-
 42, 45-60, 62-75, 140, 164
black theology. *See* African
 American theology

capital punishment, 155-64
"Chicago school" of theology,
 vii, 2
Christ, vii-x, 2, 3, 7, 8, 10,
 12, 13, 15, 18, 21, 33-36,
 39-40, 51, 53, 56, 58, 65,
 66, 67, 109-133, 135-150.
 151, 152, 153, 158-64
Christ and culture, problem of,
 x-xii, 135-150
Christian ethics, 151-64
church, 162-4
correspondence theory of truth,
 116-8, 120-125

deconstruction, 118-120, 125,
 130n18, 131n22, 131n23,
 131n23, 132n26

equality, 157-161
eros, vii, 80-83, 93, 101, 102
ethics, 151-64
ethics and eschatology, 33
experience, x, 4, 5, 8, 21, 22,
 32, 63, 78-79, 84, 99, 100,
 104, 105, 120-125
evil, 87-93, 100n7
 absolute and relative,
 103n23
 natural and moral, 88
evolution, x, 22, 78-79

feminist theology, 4, 8, 11-14,
 71-72, 114
fundamentalism, 38, 127

God, vii, x, 41, 77-107, 111,
 118, 129, 131n24, 140, 145,
 146, 147, 148, 149, 149n3
 activity of, 15-20, 86-87
 general and special, 87
 and evil, 87-93
 and hope, 93-99
 as Created and Uncreated,
 80-82, 101n8

as finite, vii, x, 80, 90, 93, 104n26, 146
as Person, 82-83
di-polar view of, vii, 80-82
language about, 83-86
purpose of, 87
good, the, 80-83, 100n9, 102n11
goodness of existence, 79-80

hermeneutics, 45-60
homosexuality, 37-39, 73, 140
hope 93-98
  realistic, 96-97
  utopian, 96-97

Jesus. See Christ
"Jesus Seminar", the, 115-6
justice, 152-7 159-63

liberal theology, 2, 16, 63-65
  and relativism, 55-57, 63-68
liberation theology, 8, 17, 18, 71
love, 152-63
  ethical and ecstatic, 158-61
  mutual, 152-5
  sacrificial, 152-5
  unconditional mutual 154-5
  See also, agape

marriage and divorce, 33-36
miracles, 16, 47, 104n29, 105-6n30
modernism, vii, 1-29, 32-33, 40-42, 57-59, 65-75, 151, 164

naturalistic theism, vii, 19, 22, 77-86
neo-modernism. See modernism
neo-orthodoxy, 3, 4, 16-17, 19 62

possibility, 78, 80-83, 100n4, 101n9, 101-2n10
pragmatism, vii, viii, 1-2, 6, 19, 21, 22, 70, 84-86, 99, 113, 120-4, 125, 129, 147
process theology, 4, 7-8, 17, 29
public theology, 4-7

realism, 116-8, 124-5, 130n14
  absolutist, 116, 130
  critical, 117-118, 130n14
reality, 117, 132n29
relativism, vii, 19, 51-59, 63-71, 85, 86, 110, 124, 137, 146
revisionist theology, 4-7

scientism, 102n16
theodicy, 87-93
theological method, vii-ix, x, 12, 4-15, 19-24, 25-28, 32-33, 37, 39-42, 37,-39-42, 45-75, 77-80, 109-129, 155
  formal norm, xi
  material norm, xi

GENERAL THEOLOGICAL SEMINARY
NEW YORK